CW01151407

Citroën 2 CV
with Dyane, Méhari, Ami 6/8

1948-86

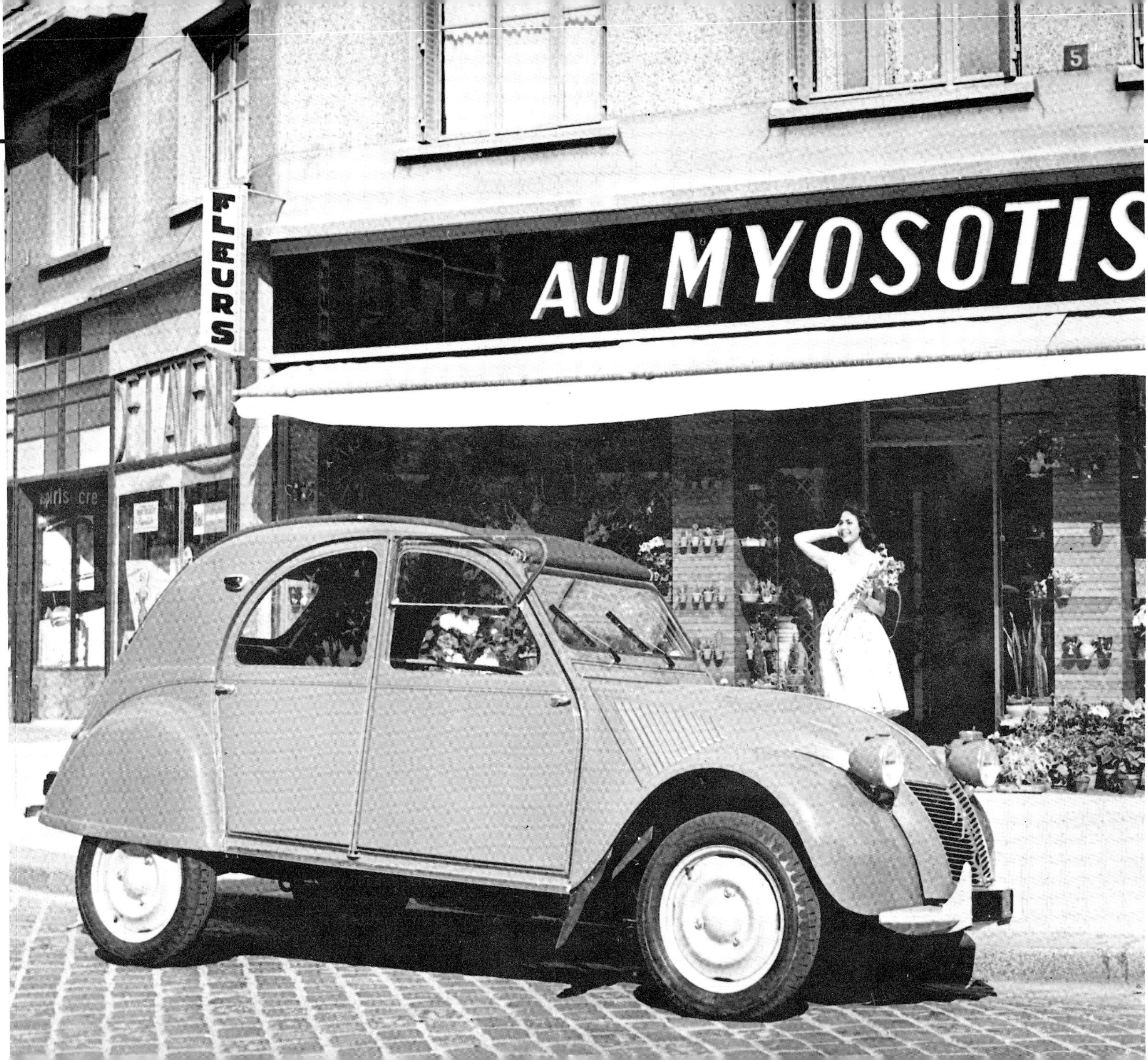
5
FLEURS
AU MYOSOTIS

Schiffer Automotive Series

Citroën 2 CV

with Dyane, Méhari, Ami 6/8

1948-86

A Documentation by Walter Zeichner

Schiffer Publishing Ltd

1469 Morstein Road, West Chester, Pennsylvania 19380

On the market for more than four decades, the Citroën 2 CV has one of the longest life spans in automotive history. In this volume of the Schiffer Automotive Series we show a cross-section of the advertising materials that have been used for the "Deux Chevaux", which, in view of its long production span, we've limited to a small selection. Memories reawaken, and many an old friend may be amused by a look back to so much uncompromising limitation which one knew how to put up with as a young 2 CV driver. In fact, the "Duck" was (and is) not without comfort, if one knows how to measure it correctly. One must be a bit of a Francophile to be able to accept the 2 CV philosophy.

This nostalgic look back over four decades of 2 CV history was made possible by many factory documents as well as the archives of Kai Jacobsen, whom we thank particularly for his support.

Halwart Schrader, Editor

Translated from the German by Dr. Edward Force.

Copyright © 1989 by Schiffer Publishing.
Library of Congress Catalog Number: 89-063365.

All rights reserved. No part of this work may be reproduced or used in any forms or by any means—graphic, electronic or mechanical, including photocopying or information storage and retrieval systems—without written permission from the copyright holder.

Printed in the United States of America.
ISBN: 0-88740-211-9

Originally published under the title "Citroën 2 CV", 1948-86, Schrader Motor Chronik, copyright Schrader Automobil-Bücher, Handels-GmbH, München, West Germany, © 1988, ISBN:3-922-617-40-9.

Published by Schiffer Publishing, Ltd.
1469 Morstein Road
West Chester, Pennsylvania 19380
Please write for a free catalog.
This book may be purchased from the publisher.
Please include $2.00 postage.
Try your bookstore first.

Contents

Umbrella on Wheels	6	Test of Courage II: Citroën Ami 8	68
Lovable Ugliness: Citroën 2 CV	12	The Little Goddess: Dyane	71
A Deux Chevaux with Two Engines	25	A 2 CV for Every Occasion: Méhari	76
The Corrugated Tin Shack: a Kombi	26	The 2 CV in the Press	86
A Little Prettier, a Little Stronger	32	Technical Data 1948-86	88
Test of Courage: Citroën Ami 6	61	Literature for the 2 CV Fan	95

Umbrella on Wheels

The Citroën 2 CV holds a special position among all the world's cars, for the Duck is now in its fortieth year of production and is the only production "oldtimer" that one can still buy new today.

In our day of four-valve cylinder heads, turbochargers and digitalized dashboards, there is still an automobile with heavy Thirties style fenders, free-standing headlights, that were slowly going out of style even then, and a little two-cylinder engine of less than 30 HP. People buy this car in respectable numbers, that at the most goes, barely over 100 kph, and not because of poverty or ignorance, no, they feel especially good in this four-wheeled anachronism that hurries through curves shaking and tilting scarily on its thin tires. 2 CV drivers have a particularly loving relationship with their car. The "Deux Chevaux" is a very special car; it leaves no one unmoved.

Since the beginning, many more than five million of these "prehistoric" vehicles have been sold all over the world, as sedans or box vans, and yet these two types were only the distant ancestors of numerous other small Citroën models which were based on the 2 CV, such as the Dyane, Ami, Méhari or LN. Also, there were numerous crazy and exotic relatives of the "Duck", like the twin-engined Sahara type or the models, as good as unknown here, that were made under license in other countries, such as the British Bijou or Pick Up, the Spanish FAF, Vietnamese Dalat or Persian Baby Brousse, to name a few.

The 2 CV and its kin were, and in part still are, produced in twenty countries on this earth, from England to Vietnam and Uruguay to the Ivory Coast. If production were to stop, which would sadden many, it surely would not be the end.

The origin of the 2 CV is found in France during the Thirties, when Citroën chief Pierre Boulanger realized there was a great need for a cheap, roomy and undemanding vehicle in his country. In an agrarian land like France, dominated by Paris as the only big city, a car for the farmer who wanted to bring his produce to market, or for the artisan, country doctor or parish priest, had to be a real blessing. As long as it was inexpensive and simple, every owner could get along with it without problems. Boulanger came to the conclusion that such a car should only be capable of moving two people and 50 kilograms of goods at a speed of about 60 kph, even over bad roads. Also, if possible, it wouldn't consume more than three liters of fuel in 100 kilometers. The appearance of the car was of little importance; the price was more important and should, if possible, amount to no more than one-third that of the "Gangster" Citroën 11 CV Traction Avant. Soon afterward, serious work began on this "TPV" (toute petite voiture (very small car)) project. One can well imagine the strange feeling of the later DS designer Flaminio Bertoni when he was given the contract to design a car whose appearance was of no importance, and malicious types still like to say that this is the reason for the 2 CV's unusual appearance.

Early in 1937 the first prototype rolled out of the testing department. The car was already characterized with strange features. The springing was done by torsion bars, the doors were semicircular, and the canvas seats resembled hammocks. Since there was as yet no suitable Citroën engine available, a 500-cc BMW motorcycle motor served as its temporary powerplant.

All in all, the test model met Boulanger's requirements, for the springing proved to be comfortable enough to transport a basket of raw eggs over a rough country road without breaking a single egg. Tests now began with a one-cylinder engine of Citroën's own construction, but was too weak and finally caught fire, destroying one of the test cars. Relying on the BMW boxer, there soon appeared a water-cooled two-cylinder engine of 375-cc displacement, behind which was installed a radiator from the 11 CV.

By the end of 1937, some twenty cars, most of them without a real body, were being tested. The drivers wore leather aviation jackets in the winter in order to stand the cold. Several problems in particular were the springs, which let the ground clearance decrease too quickly under pressure, and the welding of the aluminum body parts, which could not be done satisfactorily. Despite these problems, in the Summer of 1938 Boulanger was all for starting series production as soon as possible, and scheduled it to begin in May of 1939. But the work on production models in Levallois, where the Citroën trucks and buses were built, was prolonged by several problems, so that the first TPV car did not leave the factory until September 2, 1939.

Even the unattractive 2 CV of today looks like a real beauty when compared to the "ancestress" of all Citroën Ducks. To be sure, one can immediately recognize the basic form of the postwar 2 CV in this long-legged primitive vehicle, but the two are still

Above and left: Citroën 2 CV of 1960.

Right: Steering wheel of the 2 CV Type AZL of September 1962.

2 CV Sahara with two
enginges, recognizable by the
spare wheel on the front
hood.

Now with a new face:
1962 2 CV as a delivery van
(Camionette).

worlds apart. From the deeply ribbed front end with its rectangular engine hood lying via naked door flaps to the interior, and with the back of the front seat bench hanging on steel wires, and also the shift lever sticking out of the firewall, the picture was one of uncompromising primitivism. It can be regarded as a stroke of luck for the Citroën firm that this Spartan car was never put into series production, much less put on sale, for it was anything but developed. But on the very next day Germany declared war on France and all work on the TPV stopped immediately.

During the occupation, the Germans showed a lively interest in the TPV, but Boulanger strictly forbade any cooperation and even had the remaining production cars destroyed.

He secretly believed the war would end soon and had the car developed as much as possible. This applied especially to the body and engine, which proved to be very unwilling to start at low temperatures. Toward the end of the war, several prototypes had a central headlight in the middle of the hood, and a sheet steel body had been adopted again. Constructor Walter Becchia, who had come to Citröen from Talbot, worked on the engine and gearbox, rebuilding the 375-cc engine. The new engine was designed for simplicity, and was to be air-cooled, and also, a fourth gear was added to the transmission. This annoyed Boulanger, who would have been satisfied with three gears for the sake of simplicity, In the first 2 CV one could read an "M" instead of a "4" in the shift pattern, meaning "multiplé" or overdrive, so that Boulanger did not feel completely overruled.

After the war the work went on quickly. The body gradually took on its final appearance, with two free-standing headlights replacing the single, so that the car could not be mistaken for a motorcycle at night. The interior also looked more inviting, with genuine seat benches, a shortened shift lever and even a speedometer in the lower left corner of the small windshield. But the weight had unfortunately increased with all this "luxurious furnishing". So Boulanger had every component of the car laid out in front of him, and asked himself what was absolutely necessary. Plexiglas windows were considered, but they were not watertight, and the use of such exotic materials as bamboo and papier-maché were even considered, but fortunately not adopted. Likewise, an engine enlarged to 475 cc, and fuel injection for the 375-cc engine were given up; this would have increased the car's speed to a perilous 130 kph. Finally, at the beginning of 1948, a quick change was made; a replacement of the starting crank and the occasionally used cable starter with an electric starter, already constructed by Walter Becchia, just in case it was needed. Only small changes to the body were made—among other things, the rear fenders were made more bulbous—before three cars were displayed at the Paris Auto Show in October of 1948, where they caused a sensation.

Despite numerous critical remarks from the press, Citroën really seemed to have hit the bull's-eye with this car; more than a million visitors passed by the three mouse-gray 2 CV cars, and orders piled up quickly for the car, which was to sell at the very reasonable price of 185,000 (old) Francs. Soon guards had to be posted to protect the 9-HP cars from damage by the eager crowds. But those who placed orders had to wait a long time for their new car, which was only delivered to selected customers as of November 1949, at the raised price of 225,000 Francs.

What kind of car did the French vegetable merchant or country veterinarian get with the 2 CV Type A? The roll-up top, widely known as a sun roof and then extending over the luggage space, was actually planned for transporting cumbersome objects, but from the beginning it was one of the special amenities for the 2 CV driver. The four doors could not be locked, the seats could be removed easily, and to check the fuel level, there was a measuring rod under the filler cap. There were no directional signals, the windshield wipers got their power from the speedometer cable, or from a hand crank when the car was stopped. Whoever wanted to give a turn signal by hand had to stick his arm out the horizontally hinged side window, which could not, alas, be held in position. On the other hand, the height of the headlights could be adjusted so they would not light up the sky when the car was heavily laden and its rear end "sank to its knees".

The greatest advantages of the 2 CV were its surprising roominess and its phenomenal springing, with independent suspension on longitudinal swinging arms with free-swinging spring pots and additional friction damping on the swinging arm mounts. Four people and their luggage could actually be transported comfortably, if a bit leisurely, as the boxer engine, with its 9 horsepower, soon reached the end of its power. One sat comfortably in a 2 CV, while the people in other countries had to squeeze into their mini-cars. Despite their primitive nature, the seats were very comfortable, the big sheet-metal steering wheel was in the right position, and the originally unusual shifting could soon be handled playfully.

The roll-up roof and hinged windows provided the best ventilation, but whoever wanted to could also have a stream of fresh air from the front by opening the flap that extended over the whole car in front of the windshield. A fly-screen behind it had the job of protecting the passengers from insects that were drawn in, though the people in the front seats are bombarded with bits of bugs to this day.

One can imagine that in four decades even some features of the Duck were changed and improved. Although the present-day 2 CV itself is still almost the car it was then, it needed considerably fewer modifications than, for example, the VW Beetle.

About a year after production began, in December of 1950, the Duck was given door and ignition locks, and in October of 1952 all cars were painted dark gray instead of light gray; other colors were not yet used. As of the following summer, hoods and doors were pressed instead of welded—one can still recognize very old 2 CV cars by their welding seams.

In September of 1954 the reworked Model AZ appeared, with a 425-cc engine producing 12 more HP, making the Duck almost 10 kph faster (approximately 70 kph). One could see that on a new illuminated speedometer. Even directional lights had been added behind the side windows. Upholstered seats made the interior cozier; the lower halves of the hinged windows could now be attached to the frame instead of clattering in the wind. As of December 1956 there was a luxury version, the AZL, with thin chrome strips on the sides and hood. Rims, bumpers, seat frames and ignition switch were now set off in light gray, and the top, now made of a new plastic material and featuring a larger rear window than before, now matched the color of the upholstery: blue, green or red. Perhaps the most important new feature was a primitive defroster in front of the driver, its end piece, resembling a vacuum cleaner, ended just under the windshield.

In the fall of 1957 the car gained a sheet-metal trunk lid and was designated AZLP or AZLM. Two years later, for the first time, one could choose a color other than gray, namely glacier blue. There was even a special radio developed by Citroën for the 2 CV, called "Radioen", which was located in the glove compartment on the passenger's side.

In 1960 came the last and greatest cosmetic change to the 2 CV, in the form of a new motor hood with five respectable-looking ribs, a smaller grille and separate side panels, which spared the scurrilous car a bit of its archaic appearance. One year later the engine was upgraded to 13.5 HP.

The "Mixte" model appeared in March of 1962, with a large trunk lid, rebuilt by the ENAC firm. Now the rear seat could be folded forward, and the spare wheel did not need to be stored in the bottom of the trunk, but could lie behind the engine. In autumn of the same year, all models were given a new dashboard with a built-in speedometer and even a fuel gauge. The windshield wipers now had their own motor and were no longer driven by the speedometer cable or the driver's hand.

A new luxury version called AZAM (AM for ameliorée), with various chrome decorations and dual brake and taillights, was introduced in March of 1963. In the AZAM one could, for the first time, adjust the driver's seat longitudinally! Additional luxury details included a new plastic steering wheel and a sun visor for the passenger, complete with a make-up mirror. This year also brought a new increase in performance to 16 HP with the displacement unchanged, which meant that under favorable conditions the 2 CV was now able to reach 95 kph.

In the 1964 model year the front doors were finally attached at the front, for safety reasons. The luxury models gained a third side window, and a year later there was an automatic transmission for the AZAM version. In 1966 a 3 CV was offered, its 597-cc engine producing 21 HP, and in 1968 the basic AZL model finally had two taillights.

1970 was another year of great changes. Even the Ducks built today (in Portugal) differ only slightly from these improved types, the 2 CV 4 and 2 CV 6, which then replaced the previous models. The 2 CV 4 had a reworked 435-cc engine producing 23 HP, and in the 2 CV 6 a 602-cc boxer engine did its work, producing about 28 HP. These stronger Ducks finally passed the magic 100-kph mark.

Rectangular headlights and small metal plates with the model designation instead of the old flowing chrome letters were changes of the 1974 model year. when a rolling/folding top, opening from inside, was also introduced. In 1975 the 2 CV 6's power was limited to 26 HP because of strict exhaust regulations, and in the following year the 2 CV Spécial, already available in France as of 1970, was also sold in Germany; it was a nostalgic or thrifty version with the look of the early Sixties, without a third side window, and with the old dashboard, round headlights and simpler interior furnishings. In 1978, the production of the 435-cm engine ended, and the Spécial was given the engine of the 2 CV 6 as well as a third side window, and was now renamed the 2 CV 6 Spécial. There was also—and remains to this day—the 2 CV Club, with high-quality furnishings. The last technical revolution was in 1981, when inside front disc brakes were installed; one could also get a centrifugal clutch optionally.

Over the years there were also several more or less jolly special versions of the 2 CV, such as the noticeable orange-and-white speckled SPOT of 1976, of which 1800 were made, or the 007 Duck with bullet-hole patches on the body and huge "James Bond 007" signs on the sides, of which 300 were built, all painted yellow. In 1980 the Charleston Duck, still very popular today, was introduced. At first planned as a limited edition, this very lovingly and tastefully equipped "Noble Duck" quickly became so popular that it has held a regular place in production to this day.

Other members of the big 2 CV family are the AU sheet-metal box van Ducks built in France from 1951 to 1978 and always lagging behind the sedan in terms of development. In the English Citroën factory at Slough, there was even a pick-up truck version built independently and used in the army. The British gave the 2 CV's, built under license there, a personality of their own, for example, hinged rear windows and even a dynamic radiator figure for the sedan. They also built a 2 CV called the "Bijou" in the early Sixties, with a plastic body, but it attracted little interest and only 213 were built.

Without a doubt, the most spectacular 2 CV was that built in Vigo, Spain between 1957 and 1967 as well as by the firm of Panhard, which was soon to be absorbed by Citroën: the "Sahara", a 4x4 with two engines for front and rear drive. This off-road model had a gearbox with central shift and two clutches, and could also be driven on either the front or the rear engine. The adventurous character of this model, which could attain a good 100 kph with its two 12.5-HP engines and could climb even gigantic sand dunes without trouble, was easily recognized by the spare wheel on the front hood and rear wheel cutouts.

Turning to the more distant relatives of the 2 CV, we find that the story begins in 1961 with the introduction of the Ami 6, which had the same

Text continued on page 94.

Lovable Ugliness: 2 CV

The Deux Chevaux—so called because of its tax horsepower—was not beautiful but striking and unmistakable from the start. The form and design were maintained consistently for decades.

Early brochure pages in German, produced for Austria and Switzerland. In the Kombi there was only one seat!

THE CITROEN 2 CV
"Front drive"
4 seats and 4 doors
One feels good—for there is plenty of space.
The "2 CV" is a real car. Four people can sit comfortably in it and stretch out their legs. The softness of the seats and, above all, the new type of suspension "bridge" all rough spots in the road. The front seats are adjustable. All seats can easily be removed. A splendid advantage for camping: the easy chair is under the open sky, immediately available!
Excellently heated in winter. Splendid ventilation in summer, thanks to the regulatable ventilation flap under the windshield. By partly or totally covering the car, one creates numerous possible uses plus incomparable comfort.
One attains considerable average speeds.
With four people and 50 kilograms of luggage the "2 CV" easily reaches—on a normal road—an average speed of 50 to 55 kph; in hilly country it still averages 40 kph. The "2 CV" takes every upgrade regularly and without difficulty. Example: It achieves without a pause, fully loaded, the 22-km ascent of Mont Ventoux (1912 meters) in France.
The "2 CV" is durable.
Built to "endure". Despite its light weight, all the parts are strongly built and well dimensioned. The quality of the metal, the precision of the mechanics, the strict inspection to which it is subjected, mark it as a worthy representative of the best CITROEN technology.

LA CAMIONNETTE 250 kg CITROËN

1953

Traction Avant

French sales literature for the 2 CV. It found acceptance everywhere as a delivery van too; small businesses were excited. The competitors had only the Renault Juvaquatre and Panhard Kombi to offer.

Elle est commode

Plancher plat et portes "armoire" facilitent les chargements ; forme rationnelle ; pas de place perdue. Grande capacité : près de 2 m³ en plus de la cabine.

Suspension extrêmement douce : pas d'emballages compliqués à prévoir.

vraiment économique

5 à 6 litres aux 100 km à 40 ou 50 km/h de moyenne. Entretien facile : 4 graisseurs. Moteur à refroidissement à air, aucune précaution à prendre ni contre le gel, ni contre l'évaporation.

et d'une robustesse à toute épreuve

Sa mécanique est conçue et construite pour durer. Traditionnelle tenue de route des "Traction-Avant". La 2 cv passe partout. Freins puissants. Phares réglables en marche. Siège très confortable. Chauffage et ventilation réglables.

LA 2 CV CITROËN Traction Avant

4 places, 4 portes, et entièrement décapotable

On a de la place, on est bien

La 2 CV est une vraie voiture. Quatre personnes y tiennent à l'aise et peuvent déplacer ou allonger leurs jambes (voir au verso les cotes d'habitabilité). La douceur des sièges et le système spécial de suspension absorbent rigoureusement les inégalités de la route. Les sièges AV sont réglables. A l'AV comme à l'AR ils s'enlèvent facilement, ce qui permet de les utiliser, en "camping", par exemple, comme fauteuils de repos. Par temps froid, on est bien chauffé. Quand il fait chaud, la ventilation est réglable en marche par l'ouverture progressive du volet de pare-brise. La voiture – du fait qu'elle est découvrable soit partiellement, soit entièrement – offre des utilisations variées en plus d'un incomparable confort.

On fait des moyennes honorables

Sur route facile, avec 4 personnes et 50 kg de bagages, on tient des moyennes de 50 à 55 km/h. En pays accidenté, on fait encore le 40 de moyenne. Enfin, en côte, la 2 CV grimpe régulièrement. Elle peut, sans difficulté, franchir tous les grands cols de l'Europe Occidentale.

La 2 CV est robuste

Elle est faite pour durer. Ses organes sont largement dimensionnés. La qualité des métaux, la précision de la mécanique, la rigueur des contrôles en font une voiture digne de la meilleure technique Citroën.

"Front drive" CITROEN
Delivery Van 250 kg—"2 CV"—Type "AU"
PRACTICAL
Flat floor with "cupboard doors" make loading and unloading easier. Big cargo space that can be used to the furthest corner. Especially soft suspension: no hard jolts and thus special packing of goods is not necessary.
ECONOMICAL
The sales price is reasonable. Fuel consumption for medium average speeds of 40-50 kph: 5 to 6 liters. Easy maintenance: four lubricating nipples.
SAFE AND COMFORTABLE
Traditional roadholding of the "CITROEN FRONT DRIVE". Effective hydraulic brakes.—Rach-and-pinion steering.—Enough room for the driver.—Soft seat (possibility of installing a passenger seat.) Excellent heating in winter and good ventilation in summer.
BEST QUALITY
CITROEN technology means: Mechanical precision, quality materials, subjected to the most stringent factory inspection.

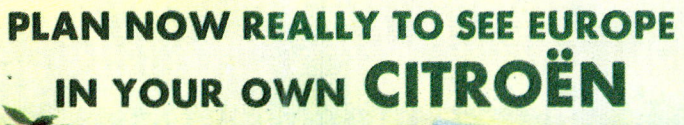

PLAN NOW REALLY TO SEE EUROPE IN YOUR OWN CITROËN

All the seats are easily removable so that they can be used as soft chairs, when camping for instance. (2 CV)

CITROËN OVERSEAS DELIVERY PLAN

...the easy, economical, convenient way to get a close-up view of the real EUROPE by private car.

Purchase in the U. S. for overseas delivery.

Resell at Citroën factory in Europe or ship back at the end of your trip.

Save more than you would if renting or shipping a car.

Avoid the inconvenience of rigid schedules, be independent of timetables.

EUROPE'S MOST FAMOUS ECONOMY CAR

A RANGE OF CARS FROM 4 to 8 SEATS

1957

Die bisher beste Lösung des volkstümlichen Automobils

* Fliehkraftkupplung
* Geländefederung
* Luftkühlung
* Vorderrad-Antrieb
* Vier Türen, 4 Plätze
* Minimale Betriebskosten

Instrumentenbrett

SICHER UND KOMFORTABEL

Vier Personen können gemütlich darin sitzen und ihre Beine ausstrecken. Die Weichheit der Sitze und vor allem die neuartige Radaufhängung «überbrücken» sämtliche Unebenheiten der Strasse. Die Vordersitze sind verstellbar. Alle Sitze können mit Leichtigkeit herausgenommen werden. Ein glänzender Vorteil für den Camping: Das Ruhe-Fauteuil ist unter freiem Himmel sofort zur Verfügung! Vortrefflich geheizt im Winter. Ausgezeichnete Lüftung im Sommer, dank der unter der Windschutzscheibe angebrachten regulierbaren Lüftungsklappe.

CITROËN

Hauptkennzahlen
2 Steuer-PS, 12 Brems-PS, Gewicht 490 kg, Höchstgeschwindigkeit 80 km/h, Verbrauch 4,5 bis 6 Liter auf 100 km.

CITROEN 425
Technische Daten und Merkmale

Motordaten: 2 Zyl. 4 takt-Boxer, Bohrung 66 mm, Hub 62 mm, 425 cm³, Kompr. 7:1, 12 PS bei 3500 U/min, max. Drehm. 2,5 mkg bei 2800 U/min, spezifische Leistung 28,2 PS/Liter.

Motorkonstruktion: Schräghängende Ventile mit Stö st. und Kipph., zentrale Nockenwelle (Zahnräder), Sieb-Ölfilter im Ölwanne, Ölkühler, Ölinhalt 2,4 Liter, 1 Fallstrom-Vergaser Solex 26 BCI, mech. Benzinpumpe, Luftfilter, Zündkerzen Marchal CR 35, elektr. Anlage 6 V, Dynamo 100 W, Batterie 50 Ah, Luftkühlung (Ventilator).

Kraftübertragung: Frontantr., Einpl.-Trokkenkupplung mit Fliehkraftregulierung, unterhalb 1000 U/min keine Drehmomentübertragung, 4-Gang-Getriebe, 4. Gang als Schnellgang, alle Gänge synchron. und geräuscharm, Schalthebel am Armaturenbrett, spiralverz. Achsantrieb, Achsuntersetzung 3,88:1 (8/31).

Untersetzungsverhältnisse: I. 25,96:1, II. 12,53:1, III. 7,46:1, IV. 5,68:1 (Schnellgang), R. 28,05:1.

Fahrgestell, Aufhängung: Plattformrahmen, vorn und hinten Einzelradaufhängung mit Längsschwingarmen, Verbindung der vorderen und hinteren Aufhängungselemente durch horiz. Schraubenfedern, vorne und hinten Trägheits-und Reibungs-Stossdämpfer.

Hydr. Lockheed-Fussbremse, Gesamtbremsfläche 448 cm², mech. Handbremse auf Vorderräder, Zahnstangenlenkung, Benzintankinhalt 20 Liter, Reifen 125×400 Pilote.

Abmessungen: Radstand 240 cm, Spur vorn und hinten 126 cm, Länge 378 cm, Breite 148 cm, Höhe 160 cm, Wendekreis 10,5 m.

Karosserie und Gewicht (trocken): Cabrio-Limousine, 4 plätzig, 490 kg.

The good old gangster car was still around, and with its expansive fenders and freestanding headlights, the 2 CV also resembled its big sisters a bit. Above: a German brochure from 1957.

15

1957

Aggressive colors, and the assertion that it reaches 70 kph on "good roads" advertised the brash convertible sedan.

CITROËN

2 CV TRACTION AVANT

TYPE AZ 425 cm3

★ Consommation : de 5 à 6 litres à pleine charge. Quelle économie !

★ Moyennes excellentes sur longs parcours : 70 sur bonnes routes, 60 sur routes variées.

★ Freins surpuissants. Tenue de route de la traction-avant.

★ Une suspension extraordinaire : ni secousse, ni vibration.

★ Bien chauffée en hiver, bien ventilée en été !

★ Air, soleil, lumière : la 2 CV est entièrement décapotable.

★ Refroidissement à air : en stationnement pendant les nuits d'hiver, pas de souci de gel ! En côte, en plein été, en plein midi, pas de risque d'ébullition !

★ Une vraie "quatre places" à quatre portes.

16

EMBRAYAGE CENTRIFUGE

Dans les centres urbains où la congestion du trafic impose généralement de fréquents débrayages et changements de vitesse, la 2 CV s'arrête et repart en douceur par le simple jeu du frein et de l'accélérateur; même en cas de fausse manœuvre, le moteur ne cale jamais.

FREIN DE RALENTI

Sur l'AZ 425, un frein hydraulique ramène progressivement l'accélérateur à sa position de ralenti, sans compromettre la marche du moteur. Celui-ci freine la voiture sans à-coups, lorsqu'on lâche l'accélérateur.

TAMBOURS DE FREINS

Les tambours sont largement dimensionnés, procurant ainsi une surface de freinage très grande.
Placés à la sortie de la boîte, ils sont bien ventilés et ne chauffent pas.
Le freinage est assuré par commande hydraulique; bien que très progressif il est extrêmement puissant.

SUSPENSION EXCEPTIONNELLE

Chaque roue oscille au bout de son bras articulé attelé à un ressort d'une grande souplesse et amorti par friction.
L'interaction des roues AV et AR nivelle automatiquement les déformations et les moindres aspérités de la route.

BATTEURS

L'effet d'inertie de la masse non suspendue entre les deux ressorts du batteur annihile le rebondissement des roues et les maintient au sol.

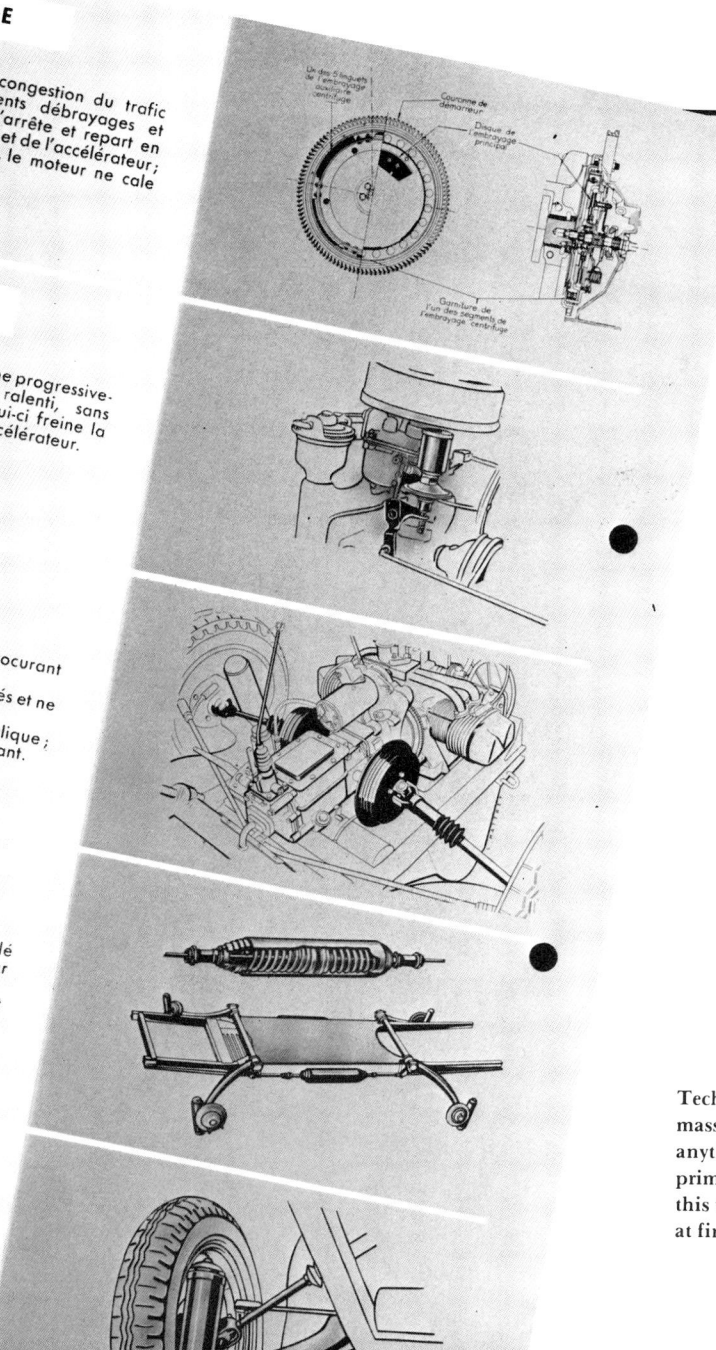

"LA PHOTOLITH" L. DELAPORTE, PARIS

Technical finesse en masse. The 2 CV was anything but a primitive car, though this was not recognized at first glance.

17

CENTRIFUGAL CLUTCH
Without disengaging, only by the simple use of brake and gas pedals, the 2 CV stops or goes. Its engine never stops, even when handled wrongly.
BRAKES
Thanks to the large brake surface and the outstandingly cooled brake drums, the hydraulic brakes have a better-than-average steady and unchangingly strong effect.
IDLE REGULATOR
As soon as the foot is lifted from the gas pedal, the regulator moves the choke vent progressively to the idling position and prevents the engine from stalling from getting too much fuel.
INERTIAL SHOCK ABSORBERS
They prevent the wheels from springing back on bad roads.
Large and comfortable interior.
Large-dimension rear window makes maneuvering easier.
Wide defroster is especially effective.

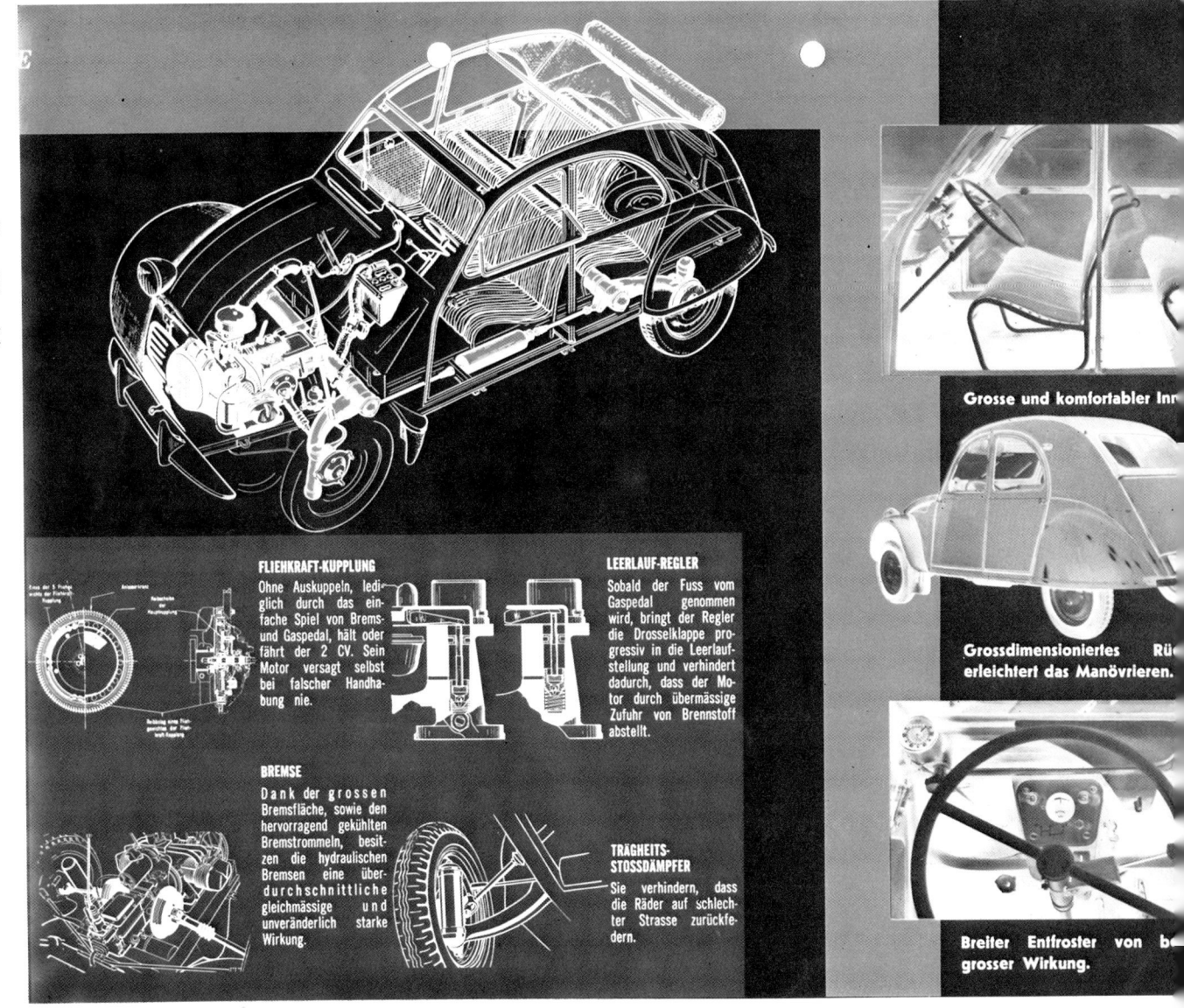

FLIEHKRAFT-KUPPLUNG
Ohne Auskuppeln, lediglich durch das einfache Spiel von Brems- und Gaspedal, hält oder fährt der 2 CV. Sein Motor versagt selbst bei falscher Handhabung nie.

LEERLAUF-REGLER
Sobald der Fuss vom Gaspedal genommen wird, bringt der Regler die Drosselklappe progressiv in die Leerlaufstellung und verhindert dadurch, dass der Motor durch übermässige Zufuhr von Brennstoff abstellt.

BREMSE
Dank der grossen Bremsfläche, sowie den hervorragend gekühlten Bremstrommeln, besitzen die hydraulischen Bremsen eine überdurchschnittliche gleichmässige und unveränderlich starke Wirkung.

TRÄGHEITS-STOSSDÄMPFER
Sie verhindern, dass die Räder auf schlechter Strasse zurückfedern.

Grosse und komfortabler Inn

Grossdimensioniertes Rü erleichtert das Manövrieren.

Breiter Entfroster von b grosser Wirkung.

SPARSAM

KOMFORTABEL

PRAKTISCH

WENDIG

SICHER

Der 2 CV verspricht und hält den niedrigsten Kilometerpreis. Er ist günstig im Ankauf und sehr gesucht als Gebrauchtwagen. Auch bei voller Belastung übersteigt sein Benzinverbrauch nie 5 bis 6 Liter. Eventuelle Ersatzteile sind sehr billig.

Die aussergewöhnliche Aufhängung gewährleistet den Insassen ein Fahren ohne jede Müdigkeitserscheinung und schont gleichzeitig die Mechanik.
Der Einstieg durch die 4 breiten Türen ist besonders leicht, und 4 Personen finden auf den bequemen Sitzen ausreichend Platz.
Der grosse Innenraum bietet, sowohl in der Höhe als auch in der Breite, volle Annehmlichkeit.
Im Sommer verfügen die Insassen, dank der ausgezeichneten Lüftung, über angenehme Frische und im Winter, dank der wirkungsvollen Heizung, über grosse Wärme.
Durch das Rolldach erhält man bei schönem Wetter zusätzlich alle Vorzüge eines offenen Wagens.

Die Sitzbänke können mit einem Handgriff herausgenommen werden; sie sind zum Beispiel als Ruhe-Fauteuils beim Picknick und beim Camping.
Der Kofferdeckel, der den grossen Kofferraum abschliesst, ist abnehmbar. Das erlaubt Ihnen, noch umfangreichere Gegenstände zu transportieren.
Das Verdeck und die Türauskleidungen, deren Farben auf diejenigen der Sitze abgestimmt wurden, sind aus solidem abwaschbarem Stoff. Zur Reinigung verwendet man, wie für die Karosserie, ein « Shampooing ».
Die Durchschnittsgeschwindigkeiten sind hervorragend (70 km/Std. auf guter Strasse).
Dank der Luftkühlung des Motors wurden Vorsichtsmassnahmen gegen Kälte oder Hitze überflüssig.

Die geringen Aussenmasse gestalten das Parkieren ausserordentlich leicht.
Dank der besonders angenehmen halbautomatischen Kupplung ist der 2 CV auch das geeignete Fahrzeug für den dichten Stadtverkehr.

Er besitzt die vorzügliche Strassenlage des Vorderradantriebs und ist unempfindlich gegenüber dem Glatteis. Die robuste Mechanik kennt keine Schwächen; sie hat dies durch harte Prüfungen in allen Erdteilen bewiesen.
Der 2 CV ist unverwüstlich, er kommt überall durch und er versagt nie.

TECHNISCHE DATEN UND M

MOTOR: 4-Takter — Zylinderinhalt 425 cm3 (66 x 62) — 2 Zylinder gegenüberliegend — auswechselbare Büchsen — halbkugelförmige Verbrennungsräume — schräghängende Ventile — Stossstangen und Kipphebel — Fallstromvergaser Solex 26 BCI — mechanische Benzinpumpe — Luftkühlung — Oelkühler — Verdichtungsverhältnis 7:1 — max. Drehmoment 2,5 mkg bei 2.800 U/Min. — Leistung 12 PS bei 3.500 U/Min. — spezifische Leistung 28,2 PS — Steuer 2 PS.

GETRIEBE: 4 Vorwärtsgänge — 2., 3. und 4. Gang synchronisiert — 4. Gang als Schnellgang — 1 Rückwärtsgang.

LENKUNG: automatische spielnachstellende Zahnstangenlenkung.

BREMSEN: hydraulische Fussbremse auf alle 4 Räder — Gesamtbremsfläche 386 cm2 — mechanische Handbremse auf die Vorderräder — vordere Bremstrommeln am Getriebeausgang.

AUFHÄNGUNG: alle 4 Räder unabhängig durch 4 Schwingarme und 2 seitliche, miteinander verbundene Federtöpfe — Reibungs- und Trägheitsstossdämpfer.

BATTERIE: 6 V, 50 Ah — Horn- und Scheinwerfer-Bedienung durch einen einzigen Knopf unter dem Lenkrad — während der Fahrt verstellbare Scheinwerfer.

KUPPLUNG: Einscheiben-Trockenkupplung mit Fliehkraftregulierung und Leerlaufregler.

LEERGEWICHT: 490 kg.

A wealth of information. At that time the 2 CV inspired a worldwide wave of empathy, jokes about it were published and grotesque records were set—as once with the Model T Ford.

EIN INTERNATIONALER SIEGESZUG

ABMESSUNGEN
Fahrzeug leer

490 kg

CITROËN

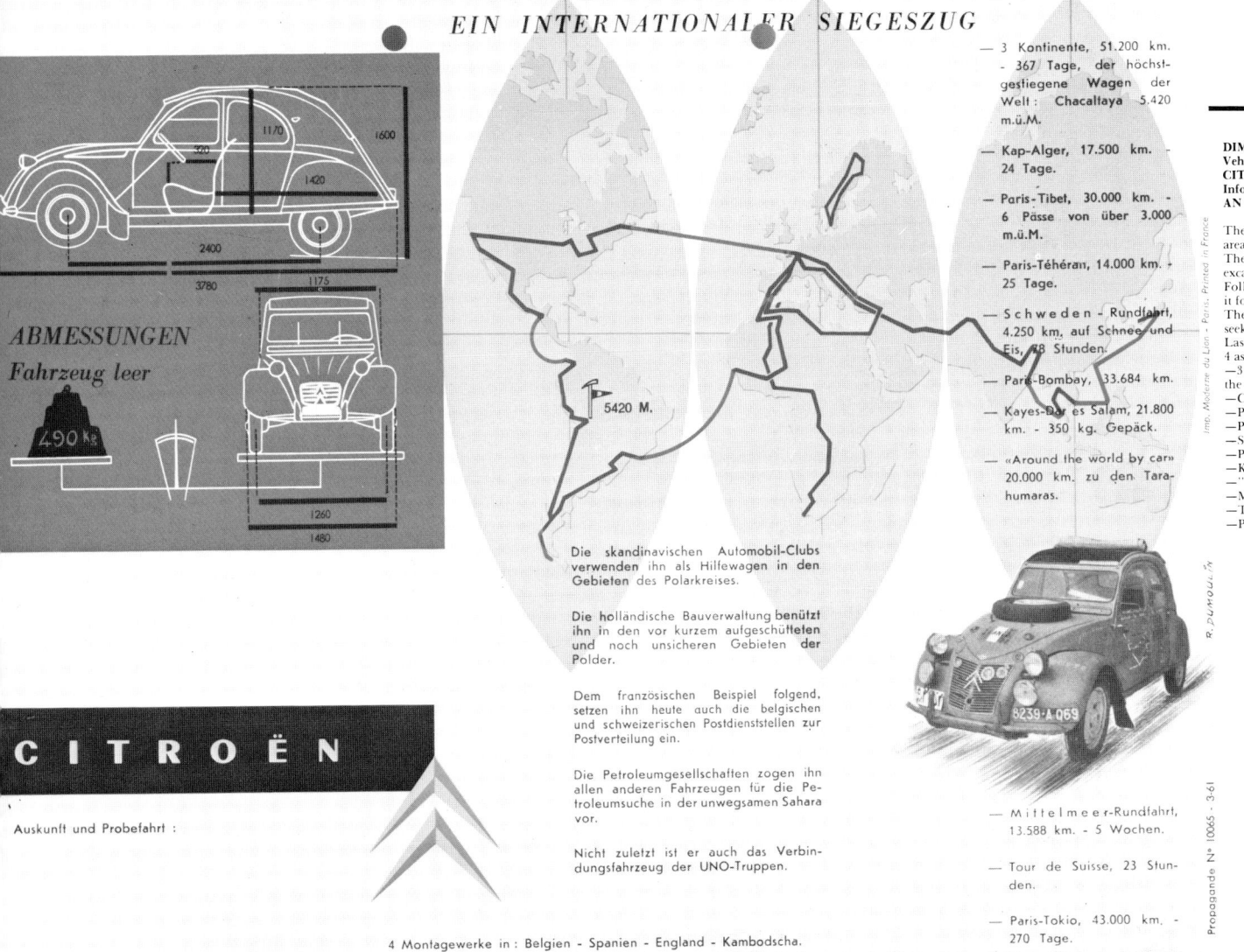

Auskunft und Probefahrt :

- 3 Kontinente, 51.200 km. - 367 Tage, der höchstgestiegene Wagen der Welt: Chacaltaya 5.420 m.ü.M.
- Kap-Alger, 17.500 km. 24 Tage.
- Paris-Tibet, 30.000 km. - 6 Pässe von über 3.000 m.ü.M.
- Paris-Téhéran, 14.000 km. 25 Tage.
- Schweden - Rundfahrt, 4.250 km. auf Schnee und Eis, 78 Stunden.
- Paris-Bombay, 33.684 km.
- Kayes-Dar es Salam, 21.800 km. - 350 kg. Gepäck.
- «Around the world by car» 20.000 km. zu den Tarahumaras.
- Mittelmeer-Rundfahrt, 13.588 km. - 5 Wochen.
- Tour de Suisse, 23 Stunden.
- Paris-Tokio, 43.000 km. - 270 Tage.

Die skandinavischen Automobil-Clubs verwenden ihn als Hilfswagen in den Gebieten des Polarkreises.

Die holländische Bauverwaltung benützt ihn in den vor kurzem aufgeschütteten und noch unsicheren Gebieten der Polder.

Dem französischen Beispiel folgend, setzen ihn auch heute die belgischen und schweizerischen Postdienststellen zur Postverteilung ein.

Die Petroleumgesellschaften zogen ihn allen anderen Fahrzeugen für die Petroleumsuche in der unwegsamen Sahara vor.

Nicht zuletzt ist er auch das Verbindungsfahrzeug der UNO-Truppen.

4 Montagewerke in : Belgien - Spanien - England - Kambodscha.

DIMENSIONS
Vehicle empty
CITROEN
Information and test drive (space for dealer's stamp)
AN INTERNATIONAL VICTORY MARCH

The Scandinavian Automobile Clubs use it as a rescue car in the po areas.
The Netherlands Construction Authority uses it in the rece excavated and still insecure areas of the polder.
Following the French example, the Belgian and Swiss post offices it for delivering the mail.
The petroleum companies prefer it to all other vehicles for petrole seeking in the roadless Sahara.
Last but not least, it is the communications vehicle of the UN tro 4 assembly plants in: Belgium, Spain, England, Kampuchea.
— 3 continents, 51,200 km. — 367 days, the highest-climbing vehicle the world: Chacallaya, 5420 meters above sea level.
— Cape to Algiers, 17,500 km—24 days.
— Paris to Tibet, 30,000 km—6 passes over 3000 meters above sea le
— Paris to Teheran: 14,000 km—25 days.
— Sweden: Round trip, 4250 km on snow and ice, 78 hours.
— Paris to Bombay: 33,684 km.
— Kayes to Dar es Salam: 21,800 km—350 kg load.
— "Around the world by car" 20,000 km to the Tarahumaras.
— Mediterranean round trip: 13,588 km—5 weeks.
— Tour of Switzerland: 23 hours.
— Paris to Tokyo: 43,000 km—270 days.

**World travels were always high in priority, especially with the 2 CV.
But it is also put to many other uses.**

1959

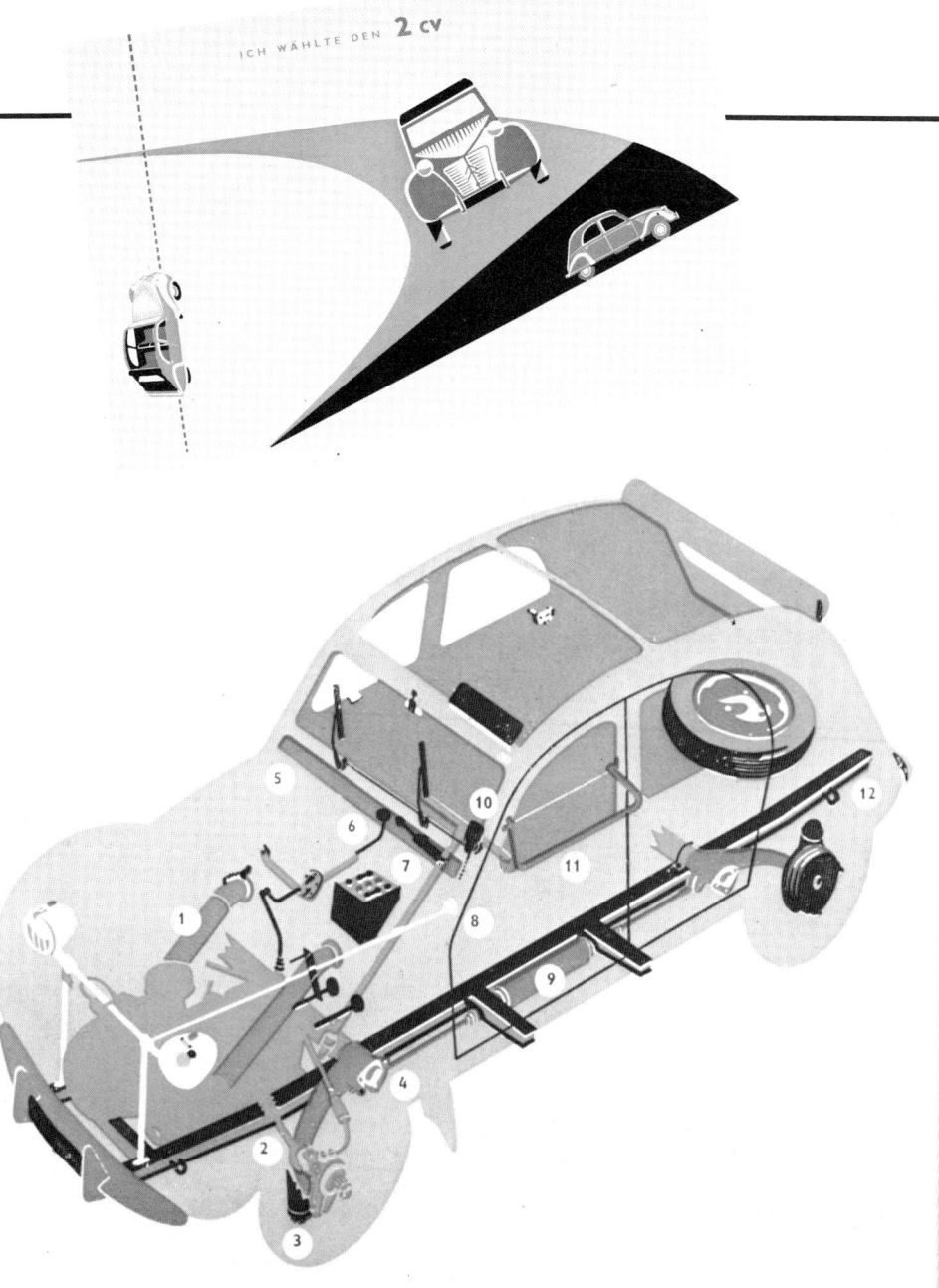

I CHOSE THE 2 CV

A color brochure produced in Holland. It was printed in metallic colors and describes the interior life of the small Citroën very thoroughly.

1. Heissluftrohr
2. Antriebswellen (Kardanwellen)
3. Trägheitsstossdämpfer
4. Reibungsstossdämpfer
5. Lüftungsklappe
6. Schalthebel
7. Scheinwerfer- und Hornschalter
8. Scheinwerferverstellgestänge
9. Aufhängungstopf
10. Kilometer-Zähler und Scheibenwischer
11. Bewegliches Türfenster
12. Fahrgestell-Kastenrahmen

1. Hot air duct
2. Driveshafts (half-shafts)
3. Inertial shock absorbers
4. Friction shock absorbers.
5. Ventilation flap
6. Shift lever
7. Headlight and horn button
8. Headlight adjusting lever
9. Suspension cylinder
10. Odometer and windshield washer
11. Movable door windows.
12. Box frame of the vehicle

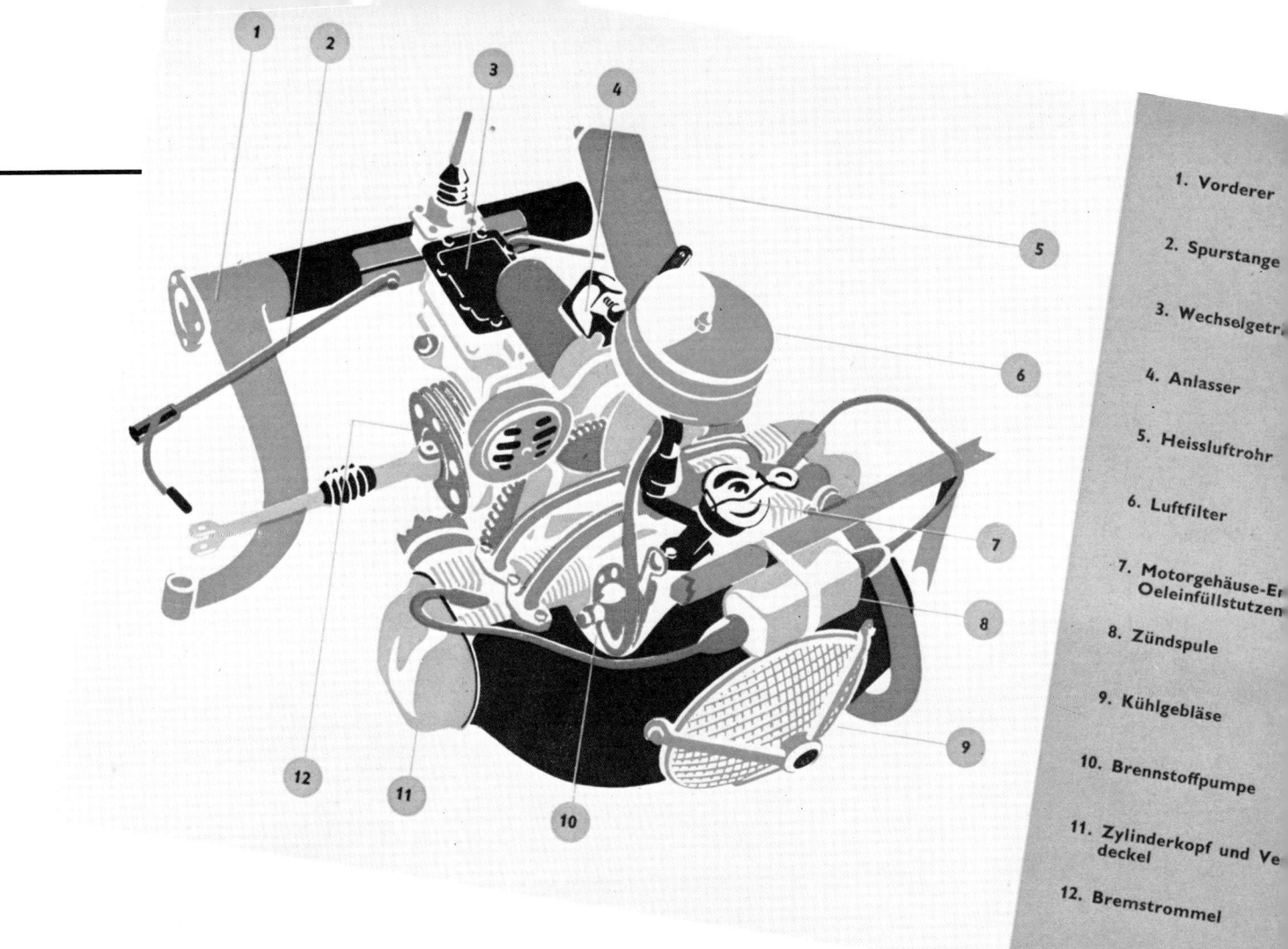

1. Vorderer
2. Spurstange
3. Wechselgetri[ebe]
4. Anlasser
5. Heissluftrohr
6. Luftfilter
7. Motorgehäuse-E[rdung]
   Oeleinfüllstutzen
8. Zündspule
9. Kühlgebläse
10. Brennstoffpumpe
11. Zylinderkopf und Ve[ntil]deckel
12. Bremstrommel

1. Front radius arm
2. track rod
3. Gearbox
4. Starter
5. Hot air duct
6. Air cleaner
7. Engine block cooler with oil fillers
8. Ignition coil
9. Cooling fan
10. Fuel pump
11. Cylinder head and valve cover
12. Brake drum

The power unit of the 2 CV, circa 1959. The two-cylinder motor had a displacement of 425 cc, produced 12 HP and was equipped with a centrifugal clutch, which automatically disengaged when the engine speed fell below 1000 rpm.

1959

An advertisement from the winter of 1959. The name "Monpti" (mon petit) was one of many given to the 2 CV—the name "Duck" as caught on all over the world, and in Switzerland the term "Zweipferder" (two-horser) prevails.

Voila: Monpti

Tens of thousands have sought a suitable name for an outstanding car. Tens of thousands participated in Citroën's great press campaign. The new name for the Citroën 2 CV has been found: Monpti*
Tenderness and respect, astonishment and admiration are included in the French pet name "Monpti". Must one not feel affection for it despite its individual appearance. Must one not admire it for its strength, its capability and its springy utility?
Yes, one must!
For "Monpti" is a genuine Citroën!
12 HP
425 cc
Tax DM 75.-
Insurance DM 90.-
Fuel consumption 4.5 liters/100 km
Standard version DM 3650.-
Luxury version DM 3950.-
The prize winners were chosen by lottery.

CITROEN AUTOMOBILES INC.
Porz-Westhoven, Kölner Strasse at the corner of Nikolausstrasse
When you inquire, please mention Auto, Motor und Sport.

1962

Technical Data

2 Motors: each with two opposed cylinders, 4-stroke, each displacing 425 cc (66 x 62), air-cooled, compression 7.5:1.
Performance per motor 14 HP by DIN at 4500 rpm. Protected by strainer oil filter.
Total power: 28 DIN HP.
Power to weight (ready to drive): 27.1 kg HP.
Power to weight (with full load): 37.1 kg HP.
2 Carburetors:
Two Solex 28 C BIN downdraft cross-country carburetors, activated by a pedal via a cable.
2 Clutches:
Single-plate dry clutches with single clutch pedal.
2 Gearboxes:
4 forward speeds, synchronized as in the Type 2 CV.
Gear Ratio:

in 1st gear	0.149
in 2nd gear	0.308
in 3rd gear	0.516
in 4th gear	0.679
in reverse	0.138

Simultaneous shifting of both gearboxes by one shift lever. A special lever allows the disengagement of the rear gearbox, so that one can drive with only the front motor (road traffic).
Transmission:
Front and rear by four universal-joint shafts.
Brakes:
Hydraulic Lockheed foot brakes, acting on all four wheels. Brake drums are mounted on the gearbox output shafts for better cooling and for protection from uneven road surfaces.
Total brake surface: 376 sq. cm.
Hand brakes with safety catch, acting on the front wheels. When stopping on sloping ground, the first or reverse gear of each gearbox can also be engaged for additional security.
Steering:
Rack-and-pinion steering. The toe-in angle of the wheels can be read from an indicator at any time (especially important when driving on sand, snow or mud).
Electrical system:
6 Volt, 50 A.h, battery 60 A·h.
Fuel system:
Two 15-liter tanks (one for each motor) and set-in leaf filters, 2 fuel pumps.
Chassis protection:
Reinforced sheet metal, with front and rear slide angles, reinforced radius arms.
Suspension:
All four wheels independently suspended by four radius arms and two linked lateral spring cylinders. Friction and inertial shock absorbers.
Weights and measures:

Wheelbase	2405
Front and rear track	1260
Overall length	3780
Overall width	1480
Ground clearance (laden)	0.160
Dry weight (without fuel)	715 kg
Dry weight (with fuel)	735 kg
Allowable gross weight	1040 kg
Top speed (on road)	100 kph

Fuel consumption per 100 km:
With both motors: approximately 9 liters (on the road), with one motor: approximately 6 liters (on the road).
Note:
For road driving, the rear engine can be turned off for reasons of economy by moving the easily reachable special lever.
If necessary, the car can be powered by the rear motor if the front clutch connection is neutralized with the help of the rod kept with the tool.

SUITED TO EVERY CLIMATE

The 2 CV 4x4 is not only suited to every terrain, but also proves itself in every climate. In cold regions or high mountains a water-cooled engine usually does not function satisfactorily: it demands at least a certain amount of maintenance, causes difficulties in starting when cold, and too little or no protection from freezing can cause damage.

For the 4x4 version, called the "Sahara", there was likewise advertising material in various languages. But this unique car remained an outsider for Africa freaks.

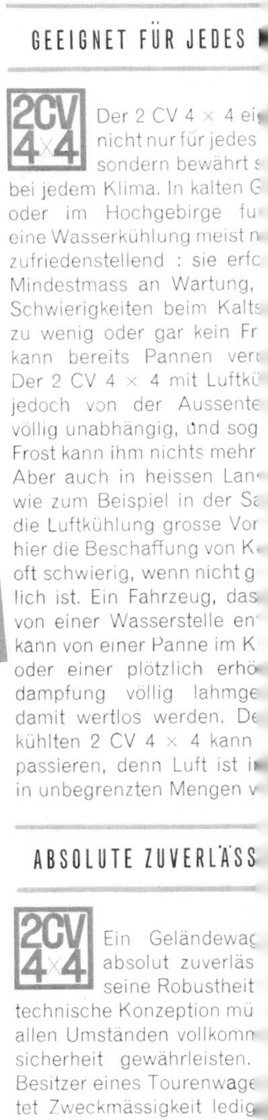

A Deux Chevaux with Two Engines

The 2 CV 4x4 with air cooling is fully independent of the outside temperature, though, and even a hard freeze cannot affect it. But in the hot regions too, such as the Sahara, air cooling has great advantages, because the obtaining of cool water there is often difficult, if not absolutely impossible. A vehicle that is far away from a source of water can be fully crippled and thus made worthless by a defect in the cooling system or a sudden overheating. This cannot happen to the air-cooled 2 CV 4x4, for air is always at hand and in unlimited quantities.

ABSOLUTE RELIABILITY

An all-terrain vehicle must be absolutely reliable: its robustness and its technical design must guarantee complete driving safety under all conditions. For the owner of a touring car, practicality means simply economy; for the driver of an all-terrain vehicle, on the other hand, it also means reliability, independence and safety.

Economy: Most all-terrain vehicles are produced in countries where fuel costs little; thus fuel consumption does not play any great role, although it naturally influences the operating costs of a vehicle. On the other hand, the 2 CV 4x4, developed in France where gasoline is more expensive, is extremely thrifty in terms of fuel consumption: using both motors, it consumes 10 liters in 100 kilometers, with one motor, about 6 liters. The higher the fuel consumption of a vehicle is, the smaller is its radius of action. What good is an all-terrain vehicle that can scarcely go far from the gas station? The work area of these vehicles is only rarely in the neighborhood of highways and gas stations.

Independence of the 2 CV 4x4 with two motors: 300 km, that means a radius of action of 150 km without having to refuel.

Safety: The direct result of the assurance of returning to the point of departure without running out of gas. Such problems—especially in the high mountains or the desert—can be fatal. The independence of the 2 CV 4x4 is even increased by the fact that it can be driven with only one motor. If you drive out with one motor and back with both, a total distance of 400 km can be covered (200 km there, 200 km back). Theoretical radius of action with just one motor: 500 km. The safety is also dependent on the type of power, especially in the mountains, on the worst roads and in the most remote areas. What security, for example, does a vehicle with only one motor offer in the desert, where one defect can be fatal? Even the best four-wheel drive is useless when an engine failure—no matter how minor (spark plug, pump, etc.) robs all four wheels of power. One must have a way out that allows one to drive on even with one defect. With two engines independent of each other, one is 100% sure. The same problem with both motors simultaneously is practically impossible. The standard for the trouble-free functioning of the 2 CV 4x4 is its mechanical robustness. The 2 CV 4x4 and the 2 CV in its normal form have the same mechanics with the original technical solutions, which are of special significance for all-terrain vehicles, which must often be driven in 1st or 2nd gear at high engine speeds. The valves, for example, cannot burn fast: they are oil-cooled. The oil system is equipped with an oil cooler. There are no problems with cylinder-head tightening, because the 2 CV 4x4, thanks to its very high degree of manufacturing precision, can avoid them.

ALL-TERRAIN VEHICLES IN LARGE SERIES

Light all-terrain vehicles have been produced in the world market previously only in small or medium series, and their final development—on account of the small numbers of vehicles—took a long time. These vehicles include an array of components that are expensive, comparatively rare and thus hard to obtain. Maintenance and repair create problems that are not always easy to solve, and the cars must often be laid up because some replacement part is missing. For that reason, such vehicles are only entrusted to experienced drivers. The wish for a light all-terrain vehicle that is always ready, economical to maintain and not chronically in need of repair, seemed at first to be a utopian dream. But the 2 CV 4x4 benefits from the experience gained with the 2 CV cars, of which more than a million have been sold all over the world for ten years. This experience assured its great performance capability, and all necessary replacement parts can be obtained without delay anywhere (and are interchangeable with the 2 CV car or delivery van). For the auto mechanic it is truly a wonder, but no riddle, simply a double 2 CV.

For the 2 CV 4x4, expensive production processes, which otherwise are used only on luxury cars, were applied: pressure casting of the engine block, clutch and gearbox housings; synchronization of the gears, etc. Since the 2 CV 4x4 is built in large series, all the advantages of 2 CV production facilities can be utilized for it, for example: precision to the micron, a variety of production inspections (260 just for a single cylinder head).

The Corrugated Tin Shack—a Kombi

The Kombi version of the Camionette, with four seats and rear windows, soon became a popular weekend and vacation car, hence this version gained the familiar name of "Week-end" even in France. Later even complete campers were offered, equipped with gas stove and wash basin in one of the back doors. The week-end was a versatile all-purpose vehicle with a minimal maintenance cost.

2 CV AZUL "Week-end"

COMFORTABLE
As you wish, it can become a comfortable 4-seater with bowed side windows or a delivery van with much cargo space.
The rear seat can easily be removed, and the right front seat can be folded frontward. The large luggage space is located behind the rear seta and is directly accessible via the rear doors.
Along with its proverbial comfort, the "Week-end" offers numerous potential uses. Thanks to the large side windows, the passengers have a full panoramic view from the front and rear seats alike. When the rear seat is removed, the "Week-end" is ready for use as a two-seat delivery truck with easy access, 2 cubic meters of cargo space, and a load limit of 250 kg.

PRACTICAL
Specially built for work and pleasure, the "Week-end" offers all the amenities of a car and all the advantages of a delivery truck. Four people with all their luggage find enough space for touring, camping or hiking and enjoy not only superb riding comfort but also great safety and a unique panoramic view.

LASTING
Especially built for transporting breakable goods, expensive special packing is unnecessary, thanks to the soft suspension.

HIGH AVERAGES
The "Week-end" has the technical characteristics of the AZU box van. It is an extraordinarily solid and indestructible vehicle. Laden with four people and 50 kilograms of luggage, it can attain average speeds of 60 to 70 kph on good roads. Thanks to its overdrive, one can attain a good 75 kph on the level. Used as a delivery van, its load limit amounts to 250 kg in addition to the driver.

ECONOMICAL
With a fuel consumption of only 5 to 6 liters it is one of the thriftiest vehicles of the present day; engine oil change: 2 liters; 4 lubricating nipples.

MOST IMPORTANT FEATURES   **CITROEN**
2 CV Type AZUL —4-stroke motor —425 cc —2 horizontally opposed cylinders —replaceable cylinder barrels —air cooling —4 forward speeds (2nd. 3rd and 4th synchronized) —1 reverse gear - 6 Volt, 50 Ah battery —headlights adjustable while driving -hydraulic 4-wheel brakes -Pilote 135 x 400 tires.
Information and test drive:

2CV AZUL   "Week-end"

KOMFORTABEL
PRAKTISCH
DAUERHAFT
HOHE DURCHSCHNITTE
SPARSAM

HAUPTSÄCHLICHSTE MERKMALE   **CITROËN**

Je nach Wunsch wird er zum bequemen 4-Plätzer mit gewölbten Seitenscheiben oder zum Lieferwagen mit grossem Nutzraum.
Die hintere Sitzbank kann leicht herausgenommen werden, und der rechte Vordersitz ist nach vorne umlegbar. Der grosse Kofferraum befindet sich hinter der rückwärtigen Sitzbank und ist durch die Hintertüre direkt zugänglich.
Neben dem sprichwörtlichen Komfort bietet der « Week-End » mehrere zusätzliche Verwendungsmöglichkeiten. Die Insassen besitzen, dank den grossen Seitenscheiben, sowohl auf den vorderen als auch auf den hinteren Sitzen eine vollständige Rundsicht. Wird die hintere Sitzbank herausgenommen, so steht der « Week-End » sofort als zweiplätziger Lieferwagen mit leichtem Zutritt, 2 m3 Nutzraum und 250 kg Nutzlast zur Verfügung.
Speziell geschaffen für die Arbeit und das Vergnügen, offeriert der « Week-End » alle Annehmlichkeiten eines Personenwagens und alle Vorteile eines Lieferwagens. 4 Personen mit all ihrem Gepäck finden für die Reise, das Camping oder die Spazierfahrt ausreichend Platz und verfügen ausser dem vorzüglichen Fahrkomfort über grosse Sicherheit und eine einzigartige Rundsicht.
Besonders ausgedacht für den Transport zerbrechlicher Waren, sind teure Spezialverpackungen, dank der weichen Aufhängung, überflüssig.
Der « Week-End » besitzt die technischen Merkmale des Kastenwagens AZU. Er ist ein ausserordentlich solides und unverwüstliches Fahrzeug.
Beladen mit 4 Personen und 50 kg Gepäck können auf guter Strasse Durchschnitte von 60 bis 70 km/Std. erzielt werden. Dank dem Schnellgang, erreicht man in der Ebene gute 75 km/Std. Als Lieferwagen verwendet, beträgt die Nutzlast 250 kg zuzüglich dem Fahrer.
Mit einem Benzinverbrauch von nur 5 bis 6 Litern ist er eines der sparsamsten Fahrzeuge der Gegenwart; Motor-Oelwechsel 2 Liter; 4 Schmier-Nippel.

Auskunft und Probefahrt

2 CV Typ AZUL - 4-takt-Motor - 425 cm3 - 2 Zylinder gegenüberliegend - auswechselbare Büchsen - Luftkühlung - 4 Vorwärtsgänge (2., 3. und 4. synchronisiert) - 1 Rückwärtsgang - Batterie 6 V, 50 Ah - Scheinwerfer während der Fahrt verstellbar - hydraulische 4-Rad-Bremse - Pneus Pilote 135 x 400.

que vous soyez...

ou   ou   ou   ou bien

et qui vous permettra de transporter n'importe où votre fragile matériel sans risque de l'endommager

A laboriously designed brochure that showed the Kombi in all its possible uses. This splendid production came out in November of 1961.

d'accès facile, d'une contenance maximum et de forme rationnelle, sans aucune place perdue

consommation minime, de frais d'entretien peu élevés et que vous pourrez amortir très facilement

Moving specialists, flower growers, chimney sweeps, caterers or jewelers—they thought of all these occupations when they planned to photograph the uses of the Kombi thoroughly.

Votre emploi du temps est chargé et vous ne pouvez pas vous permettre de panne: vous

The load limit of the Camionette was 340 kilograms.

faible encombrement, qui puisse se faufiler   partout et se garer facilement sans perte de temps

1962

The usefulness of the corrugated sheet-metal body—often made fun of—was undoubted. Only rust could do it any harm.

Un refroidissement par air

Solution moderne qui se joue de la température extérieure et vous permet de vous passer d'antigel. L'air ambiant agissant directement est l'agent refroidisseur idéal puisqu'il est toujours disponible en quantité illimitée. C'est la formule qui s'impose de plus en plus sur les voitures de petites cylindrées. Elle économise des frais d'entretien car elle permet de se passer de radiateur, de canalisations de pompe à eau, de thermostat, et de liquide de refroidissement (donc de l'essence). Elle supprime ainsi autant de sources d'incident. Elle économise du poids (donc de l'essence). Enfin, avec le refroidissement à air la mise en température optimum du moteur au départ est plus rapide.

Des batteurs à inertie

Chaque roue est équipée d'un batteur à inertie (1), c'est là le secret de l'adhérence stupéfiante de la 2 CV sur n'importe quel sol. Si vous placez une bille dans un tube que vous tenez verticalement entre le pouce et l'index et que vous baissez rapidement la main, la bille viendra toucher le haut du tube : du fait de sa force d'inertie, son mouvement vient contrarier celui que vous avez imposé au tube. Sur la route, il se passe la même chose. Ce sont les inégalités du sol qui remplacent les mouvements de votre main. Les rebondissements de la roue, organe non suspendu, engendrés par les inégalités du sol sont amortis dès le début de leur apparition par le jeu d'une masse (2) agissant en antagonisme sous l'action de son inertie propre. Cette masse liée à la roue par un ressort hélicoïdal (3) se déplace dans un cylindre creux lié lui-même à la roue.

Une suspension à interaction

Deux pots de suspension à interaction (1 et 2) relient les roues AV et AR d'un même côté dans le sens de la longueur et obligent la voiture à rester parallèle au sol. C'est un système qui permet d'obtenir sans inconvénient la grande flexibilité, nécessaire pour absorber tous les obstacles (les 4 roues indépendantes bougent alors que la caisse ne bouge pas).

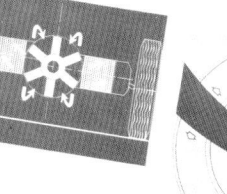

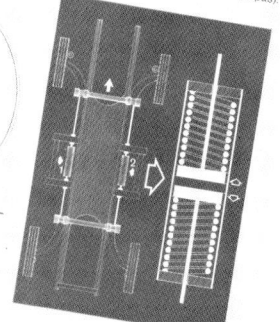

principes logiques, solutions originales

Un vilebrequin robuste

Sur la 2 CV, la technique de l'embiellage et du vilebrequin est beaucoup plus élaborée et beaucoup plus coûteuse que sur les voitures courantes. Cette technique n'est guère employée ailleurs que pour certains moteurs de compétition. Les bielles sont d'une seule pièce et complètement fermées (donc plus de vis, plus de coussinet rapporté, plus d'écrou, etc... on gagne en légèreté et en place). C'est le vilebrequin (1) qui est fait de plusieurs pièces. On n'en termine l'usinage qu'après l'emmanchement des bielles (2). Comme le vilebrequin tourne à des milliers de tours minute, il est nécessaire qu'il soit particulièrement solide. C'est pourquoi Citroën ne s'est pas contenté d'un assemblage classique mais monte les différentes parties du vilebrequin selon une technique très sûre mais onéreuse, qui met en jeu la thermique des métaux (les pièces sont usinées à la tolérance du micron, puis la partie mâle est trempée dans l'azote liquide, à – 190 centigrade environ, elle se contracte. On l'emmanche alors dans la partie femelle. En revenant à température normale, la pièce mâle se dilate et le vilebrequin est plus solide que s'il avait été forgé d'une seule pièce).

Une carrosserie fonctionnelle

La carrosserie est fixée sur un caisson d'acier, poutre plate, nervurée, sertie et soudée, extrêmement résistante et indéformable. L'architecture rationnelle de la fourgonnette 2 CV lui donne une capacité maximum (1,88 mètre cube) et entièrement utilisable. Le plancher plat est juste à la hauteur qui rend aisées les manutentions. Les parois droites ne présentent aucun angle mort. L'accessibilité est parfaite : une porte-armoire à 2 battants s'ouvrant de plain-pied avec le plancher dégage toute la largeur et toute la hauteur à l'arrière.

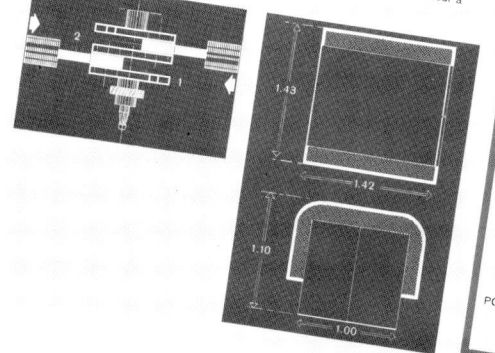

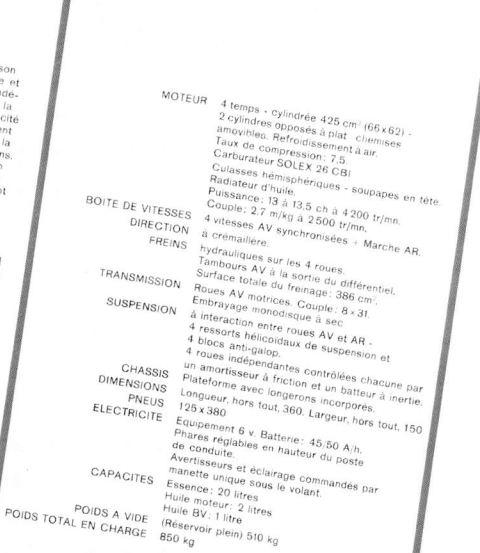

fiche technique

MOTEUR	4 temps - cylindrée 425 cm³ (66 × 62) - 2 cylindres opposés à plat - chemises amovibles. Refroidissement à air. Taux de compression : 7,5. Carburateur SOLEX 26 CBI. Culasses hémisphériques - soupapes en tête. Radiateur d'huile. Puissance : 13 à 13,5 ch à 4 200 tr/mn. Couple : 2,7 m/kg à 2 500 tr/mn.
BOITE DE VITESSES	4 vitesses AV synchronisées + Marche AR.
DIRECTION	à crémaillère.
FREINS	hydrauliques sur les 4 roues. Tambours AV à la sortie du différentiel. Surface totale du freinage : 386 cm².
TRANSMISSION	Roues AV motrices. Couple : 8 × 31. Embrayage monodisque à sec
SUSPENSION	à interaction entre roues AV et AR. 4 ressorts hélicoïdaux de suspension et 4 blocs anti-galop. 4 roues indépendantes contrôlées chacune par un amortisseur à friction et un batteur à inertie.
CHASSIS	Plateforme avec longerons incorporés.
DIMENSIONS	Longueur, hors tout, 360. Largeur, hors tout, 150
PNEUS	125 × 380
ELECTRICITE	Equipement 6 v. Batterie : 45,50 A/h. Phares réglables en hauteur du poste de conduite. Avertisseurs et éclairage commandés par manette unique sous le volant.
CAPACITES	Essence : 20 litres Huile moteur : 2 litres Huile BV : 1 litre
POIDS A VIDE	(Réservoir plein) 510 kg
POIDS TOTAL EN CHARGE	850 kg

A bit of technology belonged to the extensive information too. But the original optics of the photos was overwhelming.

31

A Little Prettier, A Little Stronger

In 1962 there was already a 2 CV model with a respectable 16 HP, in 1966 a 21-HP version, then a type with 23 HP. The Deux Chevaux grew into a Super-Duck with a respectable windspread. Special models with extra equipment were offered; the two tax horsepower had long since grown to four and six.

Happy and free

Happy and free in the 2 CV

1962

The comfort and pleasantness of the 2 CV were expressed in Citroën advertising photos like the one shown at left.

Even without four-wheel drive, the front-drive 2 CV with its brilliant independent suspension proved to be happy off the road. The car was very common in the country, and not just in France.

33

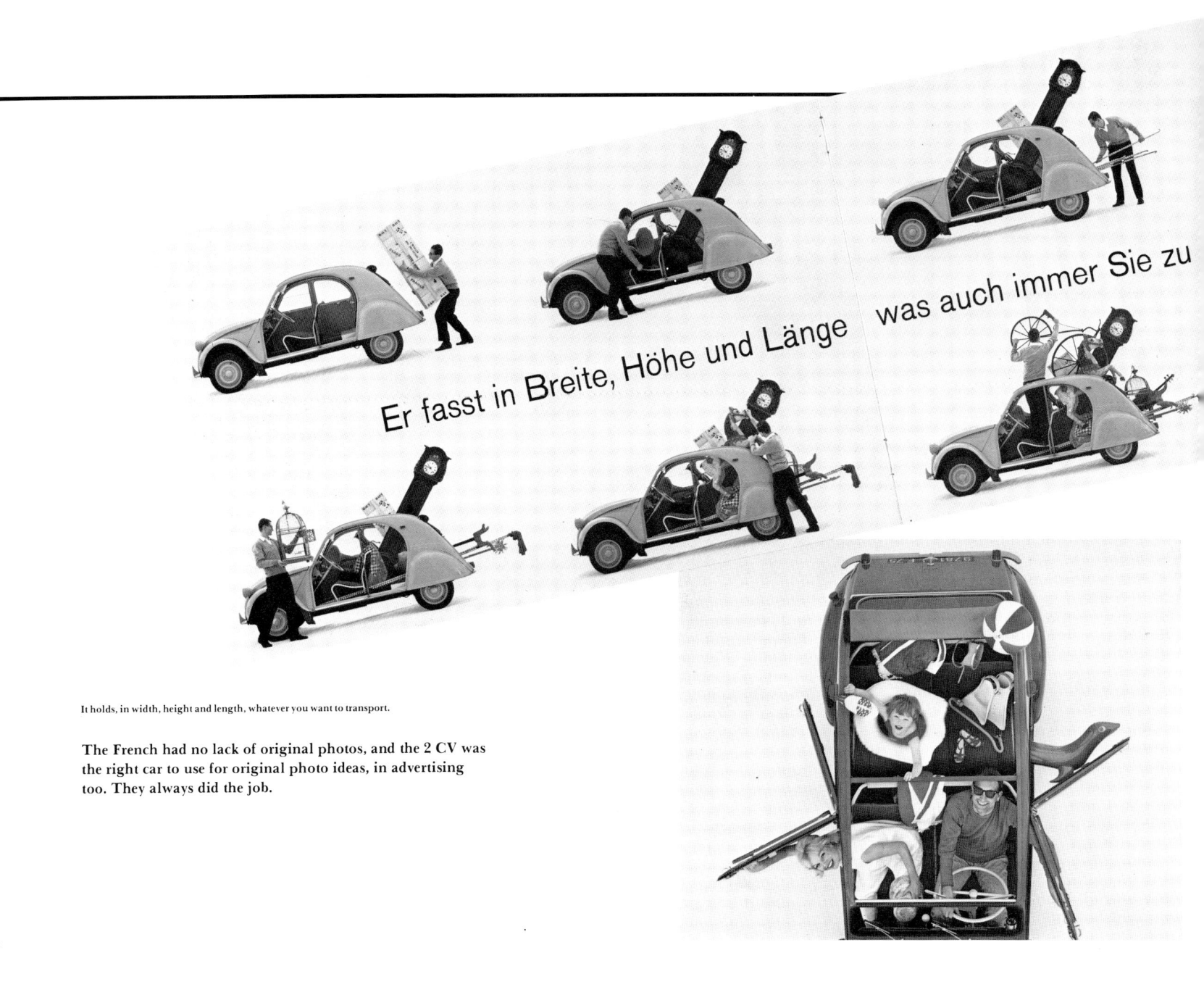

Er fasst in Breite, Höhe und Länge was auch immer Sie zu

It holds, in width, height and length, whatever you want to transport.

The French had no lack of original photos, and the 2 CV was the right car to use for original photo ideas, in advertising too. They always did the job.

...ieren wünschen

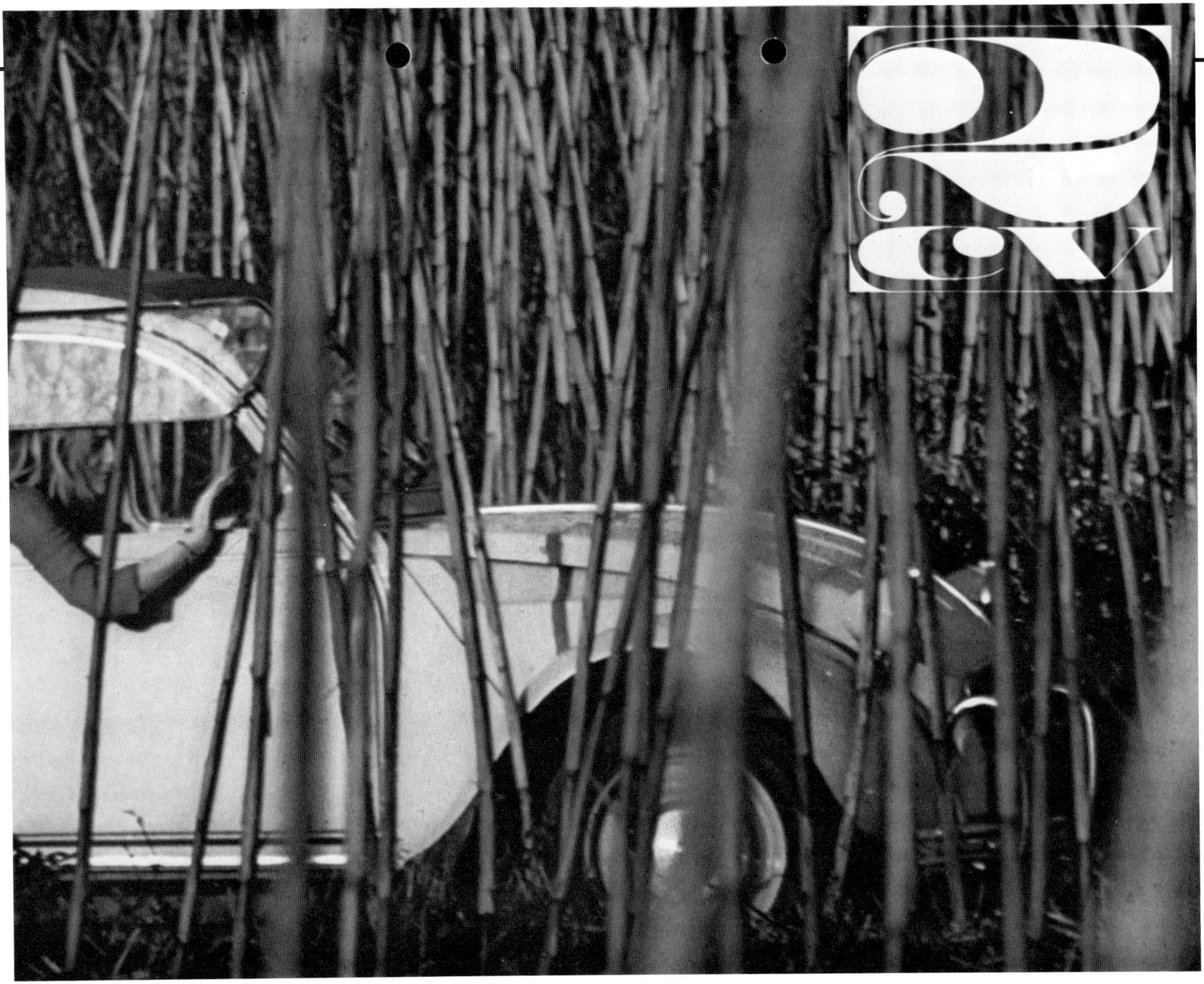
2 CV

Pictures from a 1964 autumn brochure. The 2 CV now has 16 HP, goes 95 kilometers an hour and has been refined in numerous details.

Notice the big bumpers in the form of chromed arches—a concession to conditions for acceptance in certain export countries.

37

Technical Data Motor: Air-cooled two-cylinder four-stroke opposed motor with replaceable cylinders. Displacement 425 cc (bore 66 mm, stroke 62 mm). Compression ratio 7.5:1. Solex 28 CBI downdraft carburetor with idle delay, hemispherical cylinder heads with dropped valves, oil cooler. **Performance:** 16 DIN HP at 5000 rpm. Torque 2.8 mkg at 3000 rpm. **Gears:** 4 synchronized forward speeds and 1 reverse. **Steering:** Rack-and-pinion steering. **Brakes:** Hydraulic foot brake acting on all four wheels—front brakes on the gearbox—mechanical hand brake acting on the front wheels—total brake surface 386 sq. cm. **Drive:** Front drive—bevel and crown gear 8 x 29, single-plate dry centrifugal clutch. **Suspension:** Independent suspension by radius arms and connected lateral spring cylinders. Friction and inertial shock absorbers. **Chassis:** Platform frame with built-in longitudinal members. **Tires:** 125 x 380. **Electrical equipment:** 6 Volt battery, 45/50 Ah, headlights adjustable from the driver's seat according to car's load via a button under the steering wheel. **Capacities:** Fuel tank 20 liters, motor oil 2 liters, gearbox oil 1 liter. **Dry weight:** 555 kg, allowable gross weight: 860 kg. **Dimensions:** Wheelbase (unladen) 2400 mm—front and rear track 1260 mm—length 3820 mm—width 1480 mm—height (unladen) 1600 mm. **Top speed:** 95 kph. **Fuel consumption:** 4.8 liters, according to DIN 70030. Right to make changes in construction and equipment at any time without special announcement is reserved.

38

Technische Daten

Motor: Luftgekühlter Zweizylinder-Viertakt-Boxermotor mit auswechselbaren Laufbüchsen, Hubraum 425 cm³ (Bohrung 66 mm, Hub 62 mm), Verdichtung 7,5, Fallstromvergaser Solex 28 CBI mit Leerlaufverzögerung, halbkugelförmige Zylinderköpfe mit hängenden Ventilen, Ölkühler. **Leistung:** 16 DIN PS bei 5000 U/min. Drehmoment 2,8 mkg bei 3000 U/min. **Getriebe:** 4 Vorwärtsgänge synchronisiert und 1 Rückwärtsgang. **Lenkung:** Zahnstangenlenkung. **Bremsen:** Hydraulische Fussbremse auf alle 4 Räder - vordere Bremstrommeln am Getriebe - mechanische Handbremse, auf Vorderräder einwirkend - Gesamtbremsfläche 386 cm². **Antrieb:** Frontantrieb, Kegel- und Tellerrad 8 × 29, Einscheiben-Trockenkupplung,Fliehkraftkupplung. **Aufhängung:** Einzelradaufhängung durch Schwingarme und seitlich miteinander verbundenen Federtöpfen. Reibungs- und Trägheitsstossdämpfer. **Fahrgestell:** Plattformrahmen mit eingebauten Längsträgern. **Reifen:** 125 / 380 X. **Elektrische Ausrüstung:** 6 V, Batterie 45/50 Ah, Scheinwerfer vom Fahrersitz aus durch einen Knopf unter dem Lenkrad je nach Belastung verstellbar. **Fassungsvermögen:** Tank 20 Liter, Motoröl 2 Liter, Getriebeöl 1 Liter. **Leergewicht:** 860 kg, zulässiges Gesamtgewicht: 555 kg. **Abmessungen:** Radstand (unbelastet) 2400 mm - Spurweite vorn und hinten 1260 mm - Länge 3820 mm - Breite 1480 mm - Höhe (unbelastet) 1600 mm. **Höchstgeschwindigkeit:** 95 km/h. **Normverbrauch:** 4,8 l nach DIN 70030. Änderungen in Konstruktion und Ausstattung jederzeit ohne besondere Ankündigung vorbehalten.

Right: Brochure for the AZL 3 of January 1965. The rectangular directional lights in the front fenders, and naturally the third side window, are noticeable. The front doors still open forward.

1965

azl 3

1965

The type and shape of the side windows of the AZL 3 are strongly reminiscent of a historical model: The Citroën 11 CV looked almost exactly the same.

Die Eingeborenen umzingelten uns, rückten immer näher, ihre fragenden Blicke wurden drohend, ich fixierte sie, Auge in Auge, wortlos...

Alle Segel gesetzt! Mit 75 Knoten! Kurs NNO! Mit voller Kraft voraus!

"Meine Damen und Herren, stellen Sie sich die Lage dessen vor, der zu Ihnen spricht und der sich gezwungen sah, in der gänzlichen Bedürfnislosigkeit primitiver Stämme zu leben! Ich war gezwungen, in einem gebrechlichen Verschlag zu hausen und im Wald meine Nahrung zu suchen, während ich unruhig auf die feindlichen Geräusche einer feindlichen Umwelt lauschte. So war unsre Lage an jenem Wendepunkt, als eines Tages..."

Wir schwätzen lange mit den Bauern, die gerade ihre winzigen, wie Gartenbeete gepflegten Weizen- und Hirsefelder abernten. In Nefta schliessen wir Freundschaft mit den Kamelzüchtern, die ihre weissen, braunen und schwarzen Tiere zur Tränke führen. Wir springen über zahllose kleine Kanäle, deren Wasser es eilig hat, wieder zurückzukehren zum Wasser der Erde und der Quellen. Nichts ist köstlicher, als morgens in einer Oase aufzuwachen - und genauso köstlich ist's, dort nach einem nächtlichen Spaziergang einzuschlafen. Man wird eingewiegt vom Flüstern der Blätter, vom sanften Rauschen der Palmen, vom Murmeln des Wassers.
Ich werde das in meinem Vortrag ausführlicher behandeln, mit ein paar aufregenden exotischen Anekdoten und natürlich mit Zahlen (eineinhalb Millionen Dattelpalmen, 45 Millionen kg Datteln). Aber damit befasse ich mich erst nach der Rückkehr. Jetzt lebe ich in den Oasen : überglücklich - und wunderbar faul !

The natives surrounded us, came nearer and nearer, their questioning looks became threatening, I looked them in the eye, wordless . . .
All sails set! On course NNE at 75 knots! Full speed ahead!
"Ladies and gentlemen, just imagine the situation of the one who speaks to you and finds it necessary to live in the manner of primitive tribes, completely without amenities. I was compelled to live in a rickety crate and seek my food in the woods, while I restlessly listened for the hostile sounds of a hostile world. Such was our situation at every turning point, until one day...
We talk a long time with the farmers, who are just harvesting their little fields of wheat and millet, that they tend like garden beds. In Nefta we make friends with the camel breeders, who take their white, brown and black animals to the trough. We jump over countless little canals, whose waters hurry to return to the water of the earth and the springs again. Nothing is more wonderful than to wake up tomorrow at an oasis—and it is just as wonderful to go to sleep there after an evening walk. One is rocked to sleep by the rustling of the leaves, by the soft whispering of the palms, the murmuring of the water . . .
I'll treat that more thoroughly in my report, with a few exciting exotic anecdotes, and naturally with numbers (1.5 million date palms, 45 million kg of dates). But I'll deal with that only after returning. Now I live at the oases: blissfully happy—and wonderfully lazy!

Report on an African trip in a 2 CV: This brochure of 1966 includes not only a number of excellent photographs, but also interesting (and witty) commentary that appears to have been written on the pages afterward. An evening-filling report, now very sought after by 2 CV fans.

1968

Likewise very original is the artwork of a folding brochure which, in nostalgic woodcut style, portrays a number of episodes concerning a 2 CV. The title is: "The Great Times of the 2 CV".

43

KLEINLIEFERWAGEN AZU UND AK

CITROËN

AZU Kleinlieferwagen

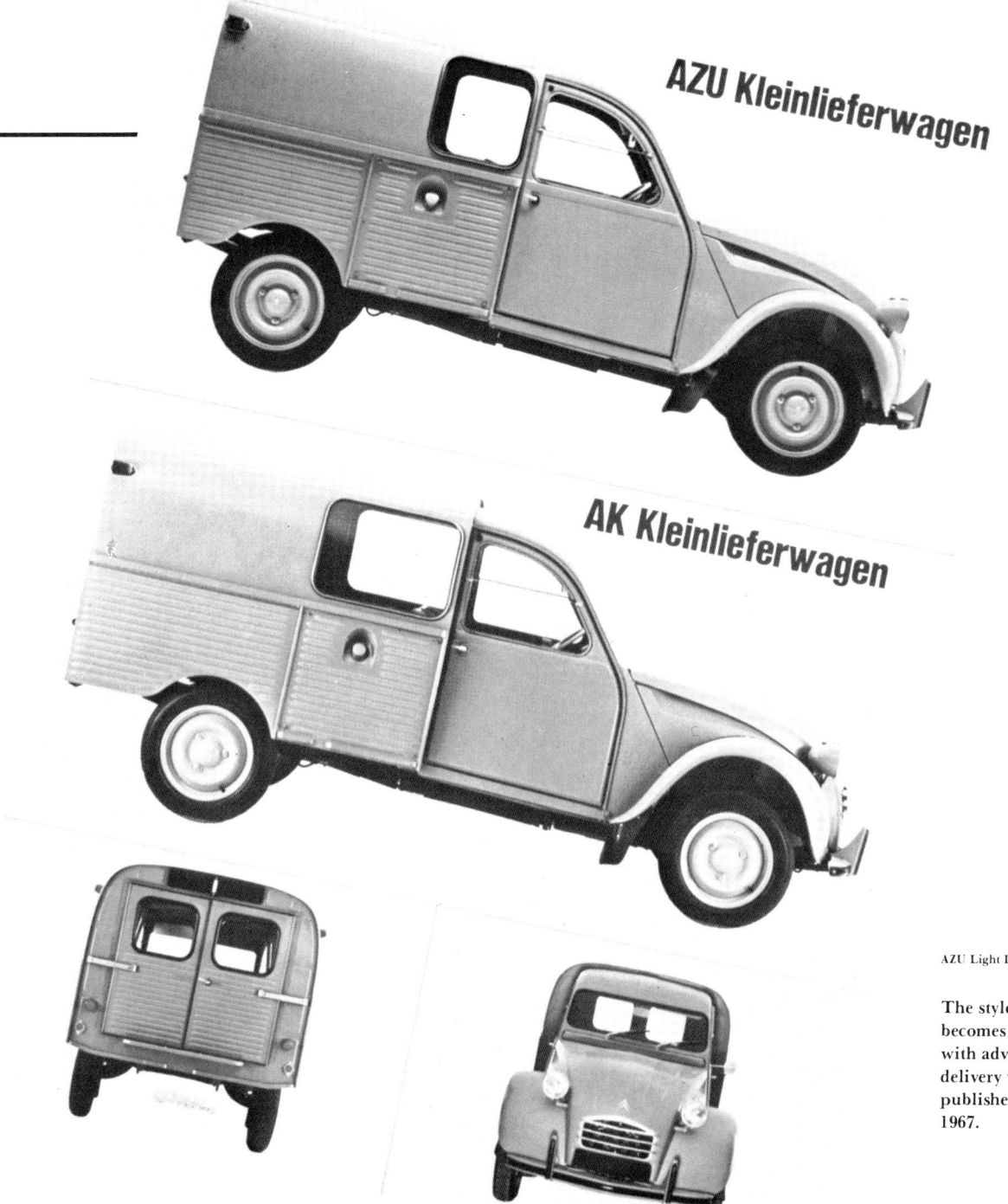

AK Kleinlieferwagen

AZU Light Delivery Van

The style of printed matter becomes simpler, less original with advancing years. This delivery van brochure was published in December of 1967.

45

1971

Six-page folding brochure for the 2 CV 4, from September of 1971. One could say that the little Citroën had grown into a "real" car.

Meanwhile the Duck has developed a proud 23 HP and 431-cc displacement, good for a genuine sustained speed of 100 kph. In its 2 CV 6 form the motor has a displacement of 597 cc and produces 28 HP.

Technical Data
2CV4

It is the car that is most suited to the needs of daily life. It interests all occupation groups and meets all demands. But above all, it is the most inexpensive French car, despite numerous improvements and considerable increases in top speed.
Motor: Four-stroke opposed motor, 431 cc (68.5 x 59). Replaceable cylinder barrels. Air cooling. Compression ratio 8.5:1. Hemispherical combustion chambers. Dropped valves. Oil cooler.
Performance: 23 DIN HP at 7000 rpm.
Maximum torque: 3.0 mkg at 4000 rpm.
Fully synchronized 4-speed transmission.
Steering: Rack-and-pinion steering.
Brakes: Hydraulic, acting on all four wheels; front brake drums next to the differential. Power transmission: front wheel drive.
Bevel crown gear: 8 x 33. Homokinetic front driveshafts, 4 coil springs, 4 suspension equalizing blocks, 4 independently sprung wheels (with inertial dampers on the front wheels). Friction shock absorbers in front, hydraulic shock absorbers in the rear. Chassis with built-in longitudinal members.
Tires: 125 x 380 X, tubeless.
Electrical system: 12 Volt rotary generator, battery 46/54 A.h. Headlight height adjustable (from interior). Single control for horn and lights near the steering wheel; electric windshield wiper.
Capacities: Gasoline: 20 liters, motor oil: 2 liters, gearbox oil: 1 liter. Dry weight: 575 kg, allowable gross weight: 895 kg. Top speed: 100 kph.
DIN-norm fuel consumption: 5.4 liters/100 km.

2 CV 6

It has become livelier, the 2 CV. On the road it passes without getting a complex. Safe, reliable, with sufficient reserve power. Thus driving is fun.
Motor: like the 2 CV 4, but displacement is 597 cc (74 x 70).
Performance: 28 DIN HP at 6750 rpm.
Maximum torque: 4.1 mkg at 4000 rpm.
Top speed: 110 kph.
DIN-norm fuel consumption: 6.1 liters/100 km.

Cloth seat covers.
Individual front seats, adjustable driver's seat.

The right to make changes in price, technical construction and equipment without advance notice is reserved.

Technische Daten
2CV4

Er ist das Auto, welches den Bedürfnissen des täglichen Lebens weitestgehend angepaßt ist. Er interessiert alle Berufsgruppen und paßt sich allen Anforderungen an. Vor allem aber ist er der billigste französische Wagen, trotz zahlreicher Verbesserungen und wesentlicher Erhöhung der Spitzengeschwindigkeit.
Motor: Viertakt-Boxer-Motor, 431 ccm (68,5 × 59). Auswechselbare Zylinder-Laufbüchsen. Luftkühlung. Verdichtungsverhältnis 8,5 : 1. Halbkugelförmige Verbrennungsräume. Hängende Ventile, Ölkühler.
Leistung: 23 DIN PS bei 7000 U/min.
Max. Drehmoment: 3,0 mkg bei 4000 U/min.
Vollsynchronisiertes Viergang-Getriebe.
Lenkung: Zahnstangenlenkung.
Bremsen: hydraulisch, auf alle vier Räder wirkend; Bremstrommeln vorn neben dem Differential. Kraftübertragung: Vorderradantrieb.
Kegel-/Tellerrad: 8 × 33. Homokinetische Gelenkwellen vorn, 4 Schraubenfedern, 4 Federungs-Ausgleichsblöcke, 4 unabhängig voneinander aufgehängte Räder (mit Trägheitsdämpfern an den Vorderrädern). Reibungsstoßdämpfer vorn, hydraulische Stoßdämpfer hinten. Fahrgestell mit eingebauten Längsträgern.
Bereifung: 125 × 380 X, schlauchlos.
Elektrische Anlage: 12 V, Drehstrom-Lichtmaschine, Batterie 46/54 A/h. Höhenverstellbare Scheinwerfer (vom Innenraum aus). Ein-Hebel-Bedienung für Hupe und Beleuchtung in Lenkradnähe; elektrischer Scheibenwischer.
Füllmengen: Benzin: 20 Liter, Motoröl: 2 Liter, Getriebeöl: 1 Liter. Leergewicht: 575 kg, zulässiges Gesamtgewicht: 895 kg. Höchstgeschwindigkeit: 100 km/h.
DIN-Normverbrauch: 5,4 l/100 km.

2CV6

Er ist spritziger geworden, der 2 CV. Auf der Landstraße überholt er, ohne Komplexe zu bekommen. Sicher, zuverlässig, mit genügend Kraftreserven. So macht Autofahren Spaß.
Motor: wie 2 CV 4, jedoch Hubraum 597 ccm (74 × 70).
Leistung: 28 DIN PS bei 6750 U/min.
Max. Drehmoment: 4,1 mkg bei 4000 U/min.
Höchstgeschwindigkeit: 110 km/h.
DIN-Normverbrauch: 6,1 l/100 km.
Stoffbezüge.
Einzelsitze vorn, Fahrersitz verstellbar.

Änderungen in Preis technischer Beschaffenheit und Ausstattung ohne vorherige Ankündigung vorbehalten.

CITROËN 2CV

小さな大もの
2CV

タイム・マシン

2CV6は今でも最初の目的通りの機能とスタイルを持っています。どうやって、この比類のない設計がファッションの移り変わった数10年間永続したのでしょうか? そして40年前より一層機能的なのでしょうか?

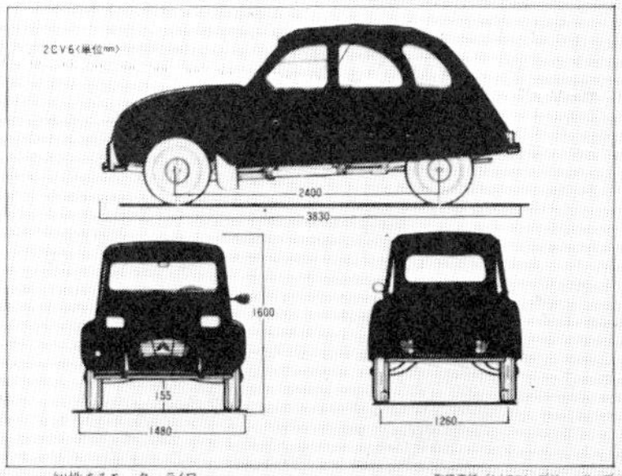

1972

な車がほしかった！

チャールストンは"粋"な面白さです。

これであなたもベスト・ドレッサー。
時代を超えた近代的なデザインは、現代のシンデレラ達が
タキシード、イブニングドレスで似合う車です。

Ⓐ ルーフは大きく開き、暖かい日にはコンバーチブルにも変ります。
Ⓑ シートはカンタンに取りはずせ、アウトドアライフに利用できます。

TRUNK ROOM
2CVの室内は驚く程広く、トランクルームも0.22立方メートルが、リヤシートを取りはずすと約4倍にすることができます。さまざまに遊びをアレンジできる広さで大モノも大丈夫。アイディアがどんどん湧いてきます

① チェンジ・レバー
② サイド・ブレーキ
③ ベンチレーター・ノブ
④ ヒーター・コントロール
⑤ スピード・メーター

Simple is Best!
優秀な空冷水平対向2気筒エンジンは、ホース類、ウォーターポンプ、ラジエーター、ファンベルトやディストリビューターもありません。各シリンダーが逆の運動をするため、エンジンバランスは素晴らしく、長時間走行もスムースです。2CV独特の関連懸架方式のサスペンションは悪路でその本領を発揮し、その乗心地は高級車に劣りません。

e champion.

In Japan too, the 2 CV got a toehold. Here is a folding brochure that was produced for the Far East and lists seven Japanese dealers' addresses. The mixture of languages also includes English and French.

2CV6CLUB・2CV6CHARLESTON 諸元表（ ）内はチャールストン

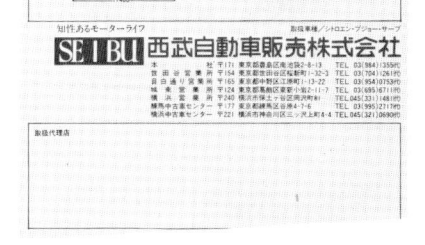

SEIBU 西武自動車販売株式会社

1972

The headlights of the 2 CV 6 are rectangular, all doors now open backward—but the 2 CV is still a 2 CV. This merrily drawn brochure was printed for the British market.

With proud words the services of the 2 CV are mentioned—not much of British understatement is to be seen here. Quite the opposite: everything is a bit exaggerated.

The safe and sure 2CV.

Get there just as quickly.
Top speed of the 2CV is 68 mph. But, if you're pressed, the average speed of the 2CV is also 68 mph. Because of its 'unburstable' engine and exceptional roadholding, you can cruise all day at top speed in the 2CV.

You'll arrive just as quickly as more powerful cars — and much more economically and comfortably than most.

Holds the road, even when there isn't one.
Roadholding of the 2CV is legendary. Not surprising because, although a simple car, the 2CV is technically advanced.

Suspension is independent all round and interconnected front to rear. Rear shock absorbers are hydraulic. Weight is evenly distributed. The car has a good power to weight ratio.

It also has front wheel drive — to pull you confidently round curves — and Michelin X radial tyres for good traction and long life.

Come rain, snow, sludge, ice, mud — the 2CV is the car which gets through.

Big brakes for quick stops.
The brakes will never overheat: they are positioned to allow much better than normal ventilation.

The drums are also of large diameter. The 2CV stops quickly and in a straight line, even on damp surfaces.

CITROËN 2CV SPECIAL

Brochure for one of the countless special versions that were always available. Here we have a nostalgic design with round headlights and the good old belt seats brought back to life.

Vive la 2 CV originale

Die Ur-Ente ist wieder da. An den runden Scheinwerfern und dem schwarzen Rollverdeck werden Sie es sofort erkennen. Auch innen finden Sie Vertrautes: die echten Leinwand-Gurtsitze.

Der 2 CV Special ist das neue Auto mit den alten Tugenden.

Genügsam wie eh und je kommt er mit nur 5,8 Liter auf 100 Kilometer aus.

Unter der Haube schlägt ein zähes Herz. Der millionenfach bewährte Boxer-Motor. Luftgekühlt.

Problemlose Technik macht den 2 CV Special praktisch wartungsfrei.

Daß er für ein langes Autoleben gebaut ist, braucht er nicht erst unter Beweis zu stellen. Seine Großväter tun dies schon seit Jahrzehnten. Treu und brav bei jedem Wetter.

Der neue 2 CV Special ist quittengelb lackiert. Damit auch jeder sieht, daß er die jüngste aller Enten ist.

Motor: Viertakt-Boxer-Motor, 431 ccm (68,5 x 59). Auswechselbare Zylinder-Laufbüchsen. Luftkühlung. Verdichtungsverhältnis: 8,5 : 1. Halbkugelförmige Verbrennungsräume. Hängende Ventile, Ölkühler. Leistung: 23 DIN PS bei 7000 U/min. Max. Drehmoment: 2,9 mkg bei 4000 U/min.

Lenkung: Zahnstangenlenkung.

Bremsen: hydraulisch, auf alle vier Räder wirkend; Bremstrommeln vorn neben dem Differential. Kraftübertragung: Vorderradantrieb.

Kegel-/Tellerrad: 8 x 33. Homokinetische Gelenkwellen vorn, Schraubenfedern, Federungs-Ausgleichsblöcke, 4 unabhängig voneinander aufgehängte Räder (mit Trägheitsdämpfern an den Vorderrädern). Reibungsstoßdämpfer vorn, hydraulische Stoßdämpfer hinten. Fahrgestell mit eingebauten Längsträgern.

Bereifung: 125 x 15 X, schlauchlos.

Elektrische Anlage: 12V, Drehstrom-Lichtmaschine, Batterie 25 A/h. Höhenverstellbare Scheinwerfer (vom Innenraum aus). Elektrische Scheibenwischer.

Füllmengen: Benzin: 20 Liter, Motoröl: 2 Liter, Getriebeöl: 1 Liter. Leergewicht: 560 kg, zulässiges Gesamtgewicht: 895 kg. Höchstgeschwindigkeit: 102 km/h. Verbrauch: 5,8 l/100 km.

Citroën 2 CV Special. Lebensfreude auf Rädern.

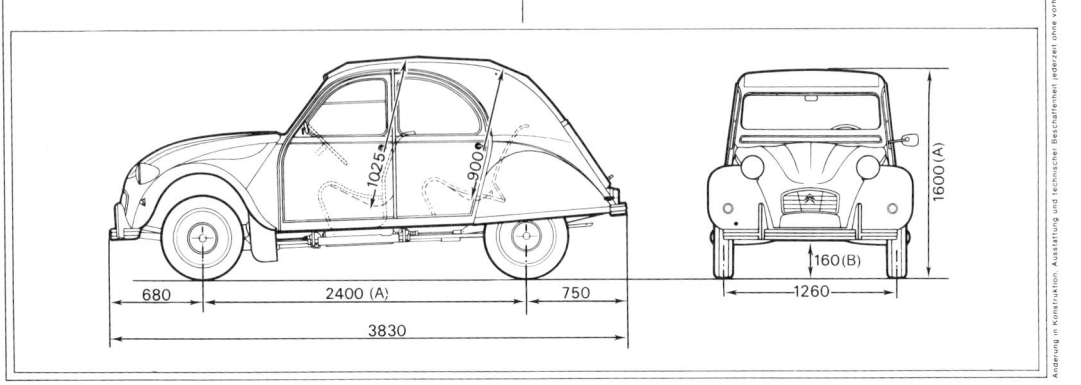

CITROEN 2CV SPECIAL
Long live the 2CV Original

The original Duck is back again. You will recognize it at once by the round headlights and the black roll-up roof. You will find familiar features inside too: the genuine linen belt seats.

The 2 CV Special is the new car with the old virtues.

As sufficient as ever, it covers 100 kilometers with only 5.8 liters.

A strong heart beats under the hood. The opposed motor, proved by the millions. Air-cooled.

Problem-free technology makes the 2 CV Special practically maintenance-free.

It does not need to prove that it was built for a long car life. Its grandfathers have been doing that for decades. True and good in any weather.

The new 2 CV Special is painted quince yellow. So that everybody sees that it is the youngest of all Ducks.

Citroën 2 CV Special
The joy of life on wheels

Motor: Four-stroke opposed motor, 431 cc (68.5 x 59). Replaceable cylinder barrels. Air cooling. Compression ratio 8.5:1. Hemispherical combustion chambers. Dropped valves, oil cooler. Performance: 23 DIN HP at 7000 rpm. Maximum torque: 2.9 mkg at 4000 rpm.
Steering: Rack-and-pinion steering.
Brakes: Hydraulic, acting on all four wheels; front brake drums next to the differential. Power transmission: Front-wheel drive.
Bevel/crown gear: 8 x 33. Homokinetic front driveshafts, coil springs, suspension equalizing blocks, 4 independently suspended wheels (with inertial dampers on the front wheels), friction shock absorbers in front, hydraulic shock absorbers in the rear. Chassis with built-in longitudinal members.
Tires: 125 x 15 X, tubeless.
Electrical system: 12 Volt, rotary generator, 25 A/h battery. Headlight height adjustable (from inside). Electric windshield wipers.
Capacities: Gasoline: 20 liters, motor oil: 2 liters, gearbox oil: 1 liter. Dry weight: 560 kg, allowable gross weight: 895 kg. Top speed: 102 kph. Fuel consumption: 5.8 liters/100 km.

2CV SPECIAL

53

1982

A well-made brochure with the 2 CV 6 as its contents, published in 1982 for the English market.

The 2 CV Dolly was likewise a special version. It had a colorful paint job and was introduced in 1985.

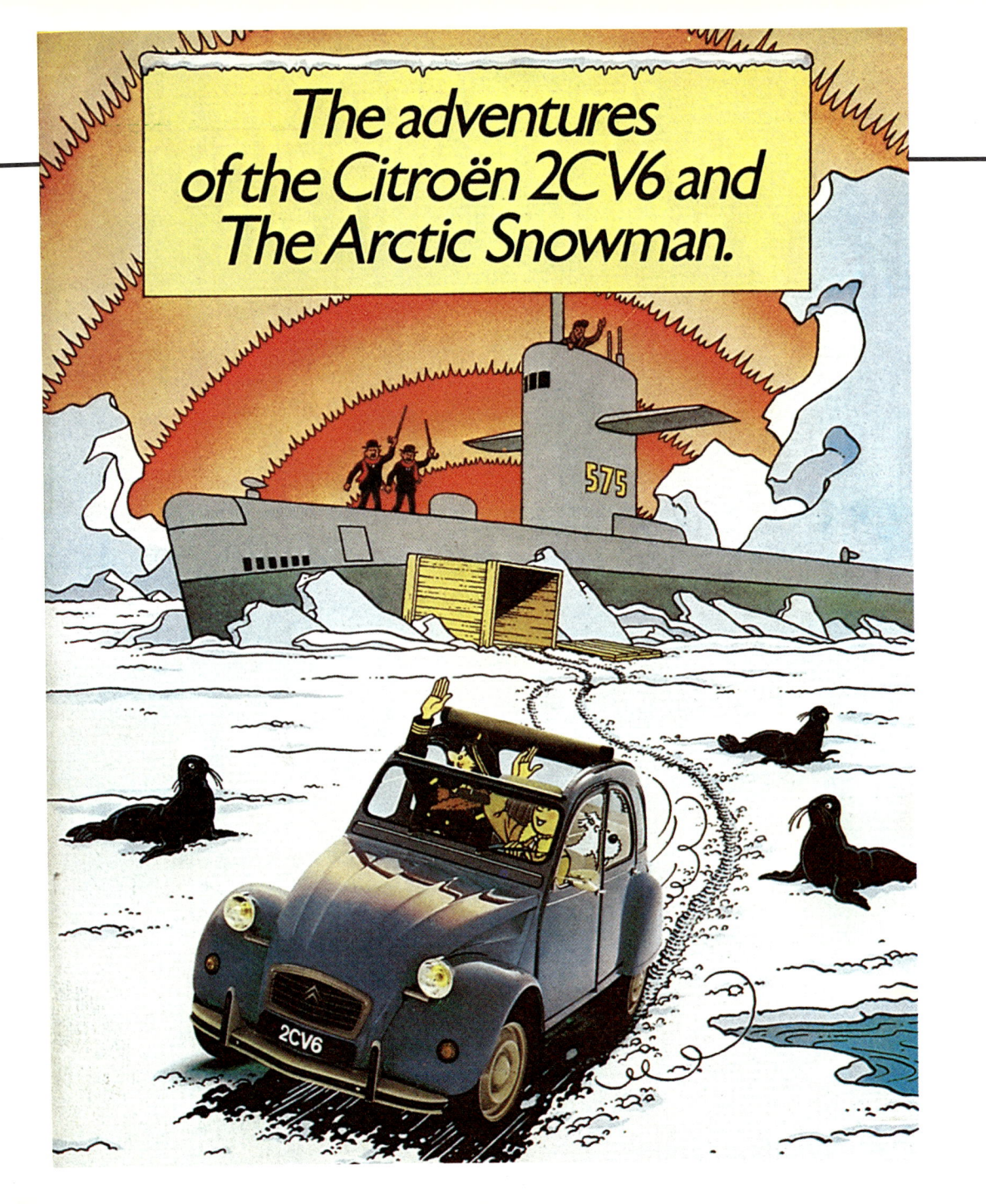

The adventures of the Citroën 2CV6 and The Arctic Snowman.

Comic figures popular in France appeared to demonstrate daring adventures in a 2 CV in this brochure. The rights to use them were expensive to buy.

Right: Inside the "Hello, Dolly" brochure shown on page 55. Such special models were always available only in limited numbers.

La Série Spéciale "Dolly" est une série folle de trois 2 CV qui fait un clin d'œil aux Stars du Show Biz des Années Folles.
Cette série spéciale est proposée en trois "robes" aux couleurs de fêtes : Gris et Rialto, Gris et Rouge, Gris et Blanc.
Bicolores, pleines d'humour, elles sont faciles à vivre ; elles peuvent par un simple geste devenir voitures de plein air, grâce à la capote qui s'ouvre à moitié ou complètement.
Ce sont des berlines 4 portes qui offrent beaucoup de place pour 4 personnes. Leur conception robuste et simple apporte la sécurité, la facilité de conduite ainsi que le confort d'une suspension originale.
Grâce à la traction AV et la suspension unique en son genre, les roues accrochent à tous les revêtements et dans toutes les conditions, rendant les "Dolly" particulièrement sûres dans toutes les situations. Avec 4 personnes à bord, les "Dolly" acceptent près de 220 dm^3 de bagages. Enlevez la banquette AR et vous doublez le volume du coffre. Cette banquette est facilement amovible.
Côté moteur, les "Dolly" sont des stars.

Pas de durite, pas d'antigel, le moteur refroidi par air n'a pas d'eau qui puisse chauffer ou geler, ce qui diminue les risques de panne. Le moteur "flat twin" d'une grande simplicité mécanique est parfaitement équilibré. Même à vitesse maximum, le moteur des "Dolly" ne fatigue pas.
Les freins AV à disque sont montés en sortie de boîte, une disposition originale qui réduit le poids non suspendu et améliore encore la tenue de route. Les 2 CV "Dolly" sont des voitures qui défient le temps, les conventions et les modes. Elles ont chacune leur charme pour mieux nous vamper ! Hello Dolly !

Les reines du Show Biz

Calais protection

At Calais, from where they are shipped to the UK, each car is given an initial treatment with Tuff-Kote Dinol while still in its protective wax coating. Only immediately prior to shipment is the protective wax coating removed and each car carefully examined for any blemish.

Tuff-Kote Dinol protection is the crown of the operation which enables the Tuff-Kote Dinol Company, in association with Citroën Cars Limited, to offer the 6-year anti-corrosion guarantee. All Citroën's UK customers benefit from this special anti-corrosion treatment at Calais. To qualify for the 6-year guarantee, owners agree to further Tuff-Kote Dinol treatments at their expense at two intervals: 12-14 months after registration, and 46-48 months after registration.

Naturally, for all UK bound cars, Citroën's concerned involvement does not stop at this. All cars are then given an exhaustive individual inspection, similar in every respect to the Pre-Delivery Inspection. The vehicles are then shipped. The repeat inspection of the Pre-Delivery exercise, now including the certified road test, undertaken just before the customer takes formal acceptance of the car, is the culmination of this remarkable series of procedures to ensure reliability. Once on the road, all Citroën cars have a 12-months unlimited mileage guarantee. This even covers the cost of roadside repairs and towing charges, if necessary anywhere in Western Europe. The first 600 miles service is free at any Citroën dealership in the UK regardless of where the car was bought. The hydropneumatic suspension is guaranteed for two years up to a maximum of 65,000 miles.

Total reliability of after-sales service from the double strength of Citroën product quality and Citroën dealer integrity

The full-life reliability of a Citroën car depends jointly on the standards of excellence built into the original product and the integrity of the Citroën dealers who sell and service it. It is a joint integrity, based on the confidence derived from Citroën's recognised advanced technology and its industrial and financial stability.

Citroën has always said that the best after-sales service is the one the customer doesn't need. Making cars with a long mileage space between services is the most important factor in ensuring that the customer is not deprived of his car. Citroën after-sales policy starts with making cars that do not require much servicing.

Assurance of the reliability and quality of Citroën cars is a joint responsibility of Citroën as the manufacturer and the Citroën dealer as the customer's liaison. Citroën has made certain that it has an ample network of sound dealers and service agents as the basis of the good service that the marque must supply. These dealers are spread over the whole country on a basis of geographical distance and population density.

So that the dealer may give good after-sales service to the customer Citroën maintains permanent training centres. Citroën is confident that its dealers and their mechanics, under constant training and advice from their own after-sales staff, have a superior level of technical knowledge, enjoy a humane and courteous customer-relationship, and that their reputation is high for the quality of the work done.

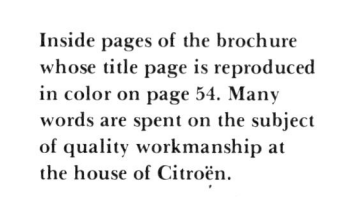

Inside pages of the brochure whose title page is reproduced in color on page 54. Many words are spent on the subject of quality workmanship at the house of Citroën.

The 2 CV and its components. Hard to believe: the 2 CV has meanwhile acquired front disc brakes.

THE CAR THAT INVENTED FUEL ECONOMY

The 2CV was designed for economical motoring- long before anyone had heard of energy conservation. It was designed to use the minimum of fuel. And to minimise servicing and repair costs. The platform chassis makes it strong and simple, without unnecessary and and expensive frills - replacement panels just bolt on. And the engine is one of the most ingenious ever made.

LESS IS MORE

The classic horizontally-opposed air-cooled twin is remarkable for what it doesn't have compared with conventional engines: no hoses, water pump, radiator, fan-belt or distributor.

Because it's flat and because the motion of one cylinder opposes the other, the engine is beautifully balanced. It is made to run at top speed, hour after hour, mile after mile.

SAFE THEN, SAFER NOW

The 2CV long predates modern preoccupations with safety. Yet in many ways it is in line with the very latest thinking.

For years it was thought that rigidity and mass were the only way to protect passengers. Now it is known that a well-designed, less massive body can actually be safer. The door locks, incidentally, are burstproof.

But the 2CV's safety record derives, above all, from its superb roadholding. Front wheel drive and the unique suspension system mean that it stays on course on any surface, under all conditions. The large wheels cut decisively through rain on the road and tyre wear is, frankly, negligible.

The braking system too, is uniquely Citroën. Front brakes are inboard, to reduce unsprung weight and improve the ride and improve adhesion. The 2CV6 now includes disc brakes with

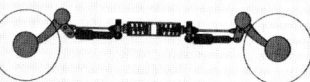

Citroën 2CV6 suspension cylinders are connected to both front and rear wheels on each side of the car. This gives it oustandingly good roadholding.

considerable stopping power which are particularly easily serviced because they are mounted inboard. There is no need to jack the car or remove the wheels. The emergency hand brake uses separate pads as a safety back-up.

ALL THIS AND COMFORT TOO

Is it paradoxical to talk of comfort in a car as frugal as the 2CV6?

After all, it does not appear to make any concessions in that direction.

But appearances are deceptive.

The 2CV6 is designed so that panels can be removed and replaced with just a spanner. The picture also shows the unique inboard brakes (now disc brakes for greater stopping power and simplified servicing) the flip-up side windows, robust air-cooled engine, removable seats and a PVC coated top.

En avant France 3!

Série limitée.

Newport 1983: Blanche et bleue, voici la 2 CV France 3, une série limitée qui va rallier tous les suffrages des supporters du Défi Français pour la Coupe de l'America.

Citroën 2CV France 3.

CITROËN préfère TOTAL

A yacht named France 3 gave its name to this special version of the 2 CV, available only in France. A part of the sales price was contributed by the factory toward the building of the yacht and its participation in the America's Cup races.

Test of Courage: Ami 6

The Ami 6 was a daring variation on the Duck theme—very avant-garde inside and out, a car for non-conformists. The sales brochures for the Ami 6 also looked different from those for the 2 CV. But this car never attained the popularity of the basic model, and replacing the 2 CV with it was quite unthinkable.

Catalog for the Ami 6, July 1964, rather cool in atmosphere.

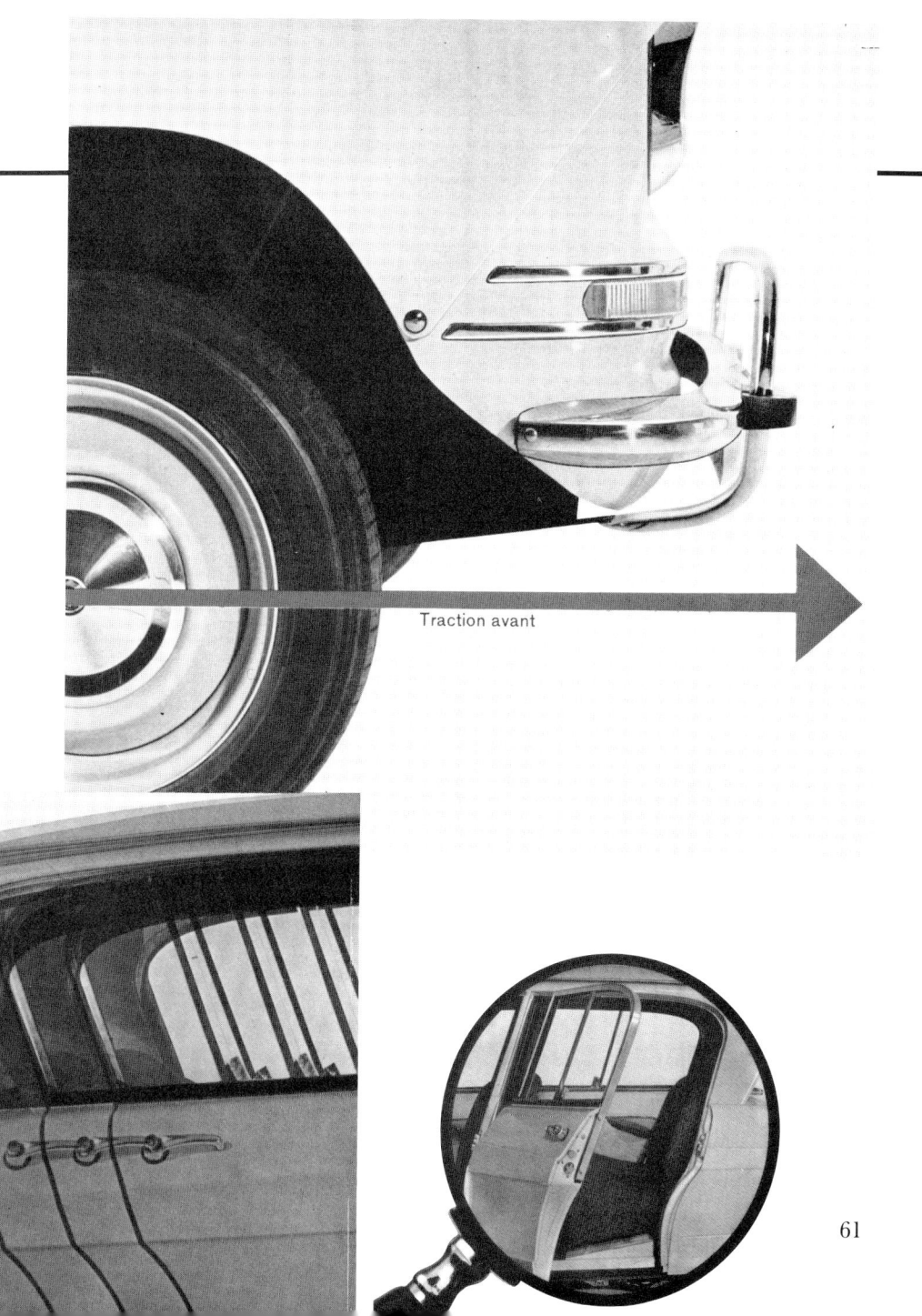

Traction avant

ami6

1963

performances

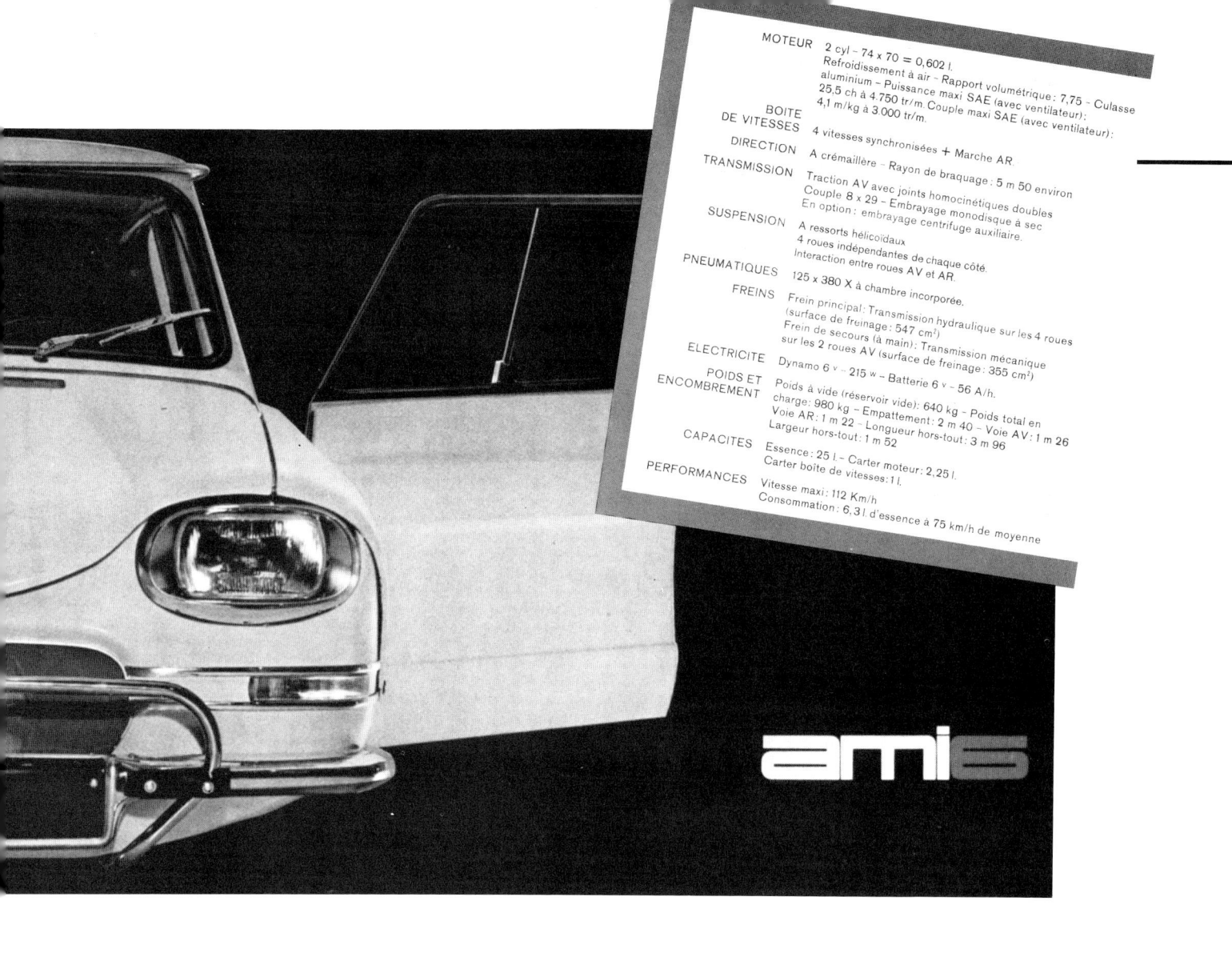

MOTEUR	2 cyl – 74 x 70 = 0,602 l. Refroidissement à air – Rapport volumétrique : 7,75 – Culasse aluminium – Puissance maxi SAE (avec ventilateur) : 25,5 ch à 4.750 tr/m. Couple maxi SAE (avec ventilateur) : 4,1 m/kg à 3.000 tr/m.
BOITE DE VITESSES	4 vitesses synchronisées + Marche AR.
DIRECTION	A crémaillère – Rayon de braquage : 5 m 50 environ
TRANSMISSION	Traction AV avec joints homocinétiques doubles Couple 8 x 29 – Embrayage monodisque à sec En option : embrayage centrifuge auxiliaire.
SUSPENSION	A ressorts hélicoïdaux 4 roues indépendantes de chaque côté. Interaction entre roues AV et AR.
PNEUMATIQUES	125 x 380 X à chambre incorporée.
FREINS	Frein principal : Transmission hydraulique sur les 4 roues (surface de freinage : 547 cm²). Frein de secours (à main) : Transmission mécanique sur les 2 roues AV (surface de freinage : 355 cm²)
ELECTRICITE	Dynamo 6 v – 215 w – Batterie 6 v – 56 A/h.
POIDS ET ENCOMBREMENT	Poids à vide (réservoir vide) : 640 kg – Poids total en charge : 980 kg – Empattement : 2 m 40 – Voie AV : 1 m 26 Voie AR : 1 m 22 – Longueur hors-tout : 3 m 96 Largeur hors-tout : 1 m 52
CAPACITES	Essence : 25 l. – Carter moteur : 2,25 l. Carter boîte de vitesses : 1 l.
PERFORMANCES	Vitesse maxi : 112 Km/h Consommation : 6,3 l. d'essence à 75 km/h de moyenne

The Ami 6 had the two-cylinder motor in common with the 2 CV, but it had been bored out to 606-cc displacement. A wagon version was available as of 1964. Production of this model ended in 1969 with the transition to the Ami 8.

citroën ami6

1963

Brochure pages from 1963, for the Ami 6.

With the AMI 6, CITROEN introduces to you an extremely practical solution to today's traffic problems: a vehicle that is completely equal to both the demands of the city and those of long-distance traffic. Its comparatively small exterior dimensions, the precision of its steering, its four fully synchronized forward speeds and—in the 1964 model— an even livelier motor (24.5 DIN HP at 4750 rpm) make the AMI 6 a handy car, easy to maneuver even in heavy big-city traffic, that gets through everywhere. The increased top speed (112 kph), which is likewise its sustained speed, its outstanding handling thanks to its front drive, its remarkable roadholding that guarantees constant contact with the road while neutralizing every bump of the wheels, likewise the extraordinary safety and comfort of its CITROEN equalizing suspension—now improved further by hydraulic shock absorbers—all this makes the AMI 6 the ideal car for weekend excursions and vacations. It is at home on superhighways as on roads of the lowest order, and in fact regardless of the season, for neither rain nor snow nor ice limit the driving characteristics of the AMI 6. Its noteworthy roadholding, its safety, its speed and its comfort make it easy for you to maintain average speeds of up to 80 kph.

Mit dem AMI 6 stellt CITROËN Ihnen eine ausserst praktische Lösung der heutigen Verkehrsprobleme vor : ein Fahrzeug, das sowohl den Anforderungen des Stadt- wie des Langstreckenverkehrs vollauf gerecht wird. Seine verhältnismässig geringen Aussenmasse, die Genauigkeit seiner Lenkung, seine vier vollsynchronisierten Vorwärtsgänge und - beim Modell 1964 - ein noch temperamentvollerer Motor (24,5 DIN PS bei 4.750 U/min.) machen den AMI 6 zu einem wendigen, auch im dichten Grosstadtverkehr leicht zu manövrierenden Wagen, der sich überall durchschlängelt. Die erhöhte Spitzengeschwindigkeit (112 km/h), die gleichzeitig Dauergeschwindigkeit ist, seine dank dem Frontantrieb hervorragende Strassenlage, seine bemerkenswerte Bodenhaftung, die einen ständigen Fahrbahnkontakt unter Ausschaltung jeglichen Springens des Rades gewährleistet, ebenso die aussergewöhnliche Sicherheit und Bequemlichkeit seiner CITROËN-Ausgleichsfederung - jetzt durch hydraulische Stossdämpfer weiter verbessert - all dies macht den AMI 6 zum idealen Wagen für Wochenendausflüge und Urlaub. Er ist auf Autobahnen zu Hause wie auf Strassen letzter Ordnung, und zwar unabhängig von der Jahreszeit, denn weder Regen noch Schnee noch Eis beeinträchtigen die Fahreigenschaften des AMI 6. Seine beachtenswerte Strassenlage, seine Sicherheit, seine Schnelligkeit und sein Komfort gestatten es Ihnen mühelos, Durchschnitte von 80 km/h herauszufahren.

ami6

1966

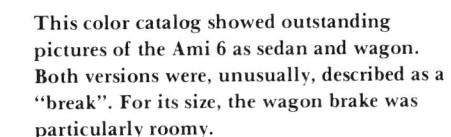

This color catalog showed outstanding pictures of the Ami 6 as sedan and wagon. Both versions were, unusually, described as a "break". For its size, the wagon brake was particularly roomy.

TECHNICAL DATA: SEDAN

Motor: Air-cooled 2-cylinder opposed motor, displacement 597 cc, bore stroke 74/70 mm, aluminum cylinder heads, compression ratio 7.75:1, performance 24.5 DIN HP (22.5 SAE HP) at 4750 rpm, highest torque 4.0 mkg at 3300 rpm.
Gears: 4 synchronized gears, 1 reverse gear.
Steering: Rack-and-pinion steering, turning circle 11.6 meters.
Drive: Front drive with dual homokinetic driveshafts. Bevel and crown wheel 29:8, single-plate dry clutch.
Suspension: 4 independently sprung wheels, equalizing springs between front and rear wheels, 4 hydraulic shock absorbers, 4 inertial shock absorbers.
Tires: 125 x 380 X.
Brakes: Main brake system: hydraulic action on all 4 wheels (brake surface 547 sq. cm), hand brake: mechanical, acting on both front wheels.
Electric system: 6 Volt generator, 215 watt, battery 6 volt, 56 Ah.
Weights and measures: Dry weight 660 kg, allowable gross weight 980 kg, wheelbase 2.40 meters, front track 1.26 meters, rear track 1.22 meters, overall length 3.06 meters, overall width 1.52 meters.
Capacities: Fuel 25 liters, motor oil 2.5 liters, gearbox oil 1 liter.
Performance: Top speed 113 kph, consumption according to DIN 70030 5.45 liters.

66

TECHNISCHE DATEN : LIMOUSINE

Motor :
Luftgekühlter 2-Zylinder-Boxermotor, Hubraum 597 ccm, Bohrung/Hub 74/70 mm, Aluminium-Zylinderköpfe, Verdichtungsverhältnis 7,75 : 1, Leistung 24,5 DIN PS (25,5 SAE PS) bei 4.750 U/min, höchste Drehmoment 4,0 mkg bei 3.300 U/min.
Getriebe :
4 synchronisierte Gänge, 1 Rückwärtsgang.
Antrieb :
Frontantrieb mit doppeltem homokinetischen Antriebsgelenk, Teller- und Kegelrad 29 : 8, Einscheiben-Trockenkupplung.
Federung :
4 unabhängig aufgehängte Räder, Ausgleichsfederung zwischen Vorder- und Hinterrädern, 4 hydraulische Stossdämpfer, 4 Trägheitsstossdämpfer.
Bereifung :
125 × 380 X.
Lenkung :
Zahnstangenlenkung, Wendekreis 11,6 m.
Bremsen :
Hauptbremse : hydraulische Übertragung auf alle 4 Räder (Bremsfläche 547 cm²), Handbremse : mechanische Übertragung auf beide Vorderräder.
Elektrische Anlage :
Lichtmaschine 6 Volt, 215 Watt - Batterie 6 Volt, 56 Ah.
Gewichte und Abmessungen :
Leergewicht 660 kg, zulässiges Gesamtgewicht 980 kg, Radstand 2,40 m, Spurweite vorn 1,26 m, Spurweite hinten 1,22 m, Länge über alles 3,96 m, Breite über alles 1,52 m.
Fassungsvermögen :
Kraftstoff 25 l, Motoröl 2,5 l, Getriebeöl 1 l.
Leistung :
Höchstgeschwindigkeit 113 km/h, Verbrauch nach DIN 70030 5,45 l.

Steering wheel of the Ami 6. Typically French, particularly typically Citroën. The DS model introduced itself.

Test of Courage II: Ami 8

The Ami 6 was replaced in the summer of 1969 by the more powerful Ami 8. It had not become any prettier, but was 32 HP strong (with 597 cc displacement). There were sedan and wagon versions of this car too. The load the wagon could carry amounted to 335 kilograms.

Left: a brochure for the Ami 8 in German; it came out in August of 1969.

1968

Parallel to the brochure shown at left, this one appeared with expanded contents. It was in glowing colors.

WHY DO YOU SAY THAT NOT EVERY DAY IS SUNDAY?

With the AMI 8 every day becomes Sunday. Even working days. Even free days. Even holidays.

A HOLIDAY LIKE CHRISTMAS

You drive away with your wife to buy presents for the children.
It is snowing. The AMI 8 laughs at snow and ice. It feels good. Because no weather can bother it.
You feel safe in the AMI 8. You buy a lot of presents. This year the children will be spoiled.
You also buy a lot of new things for the house. "But how will we bring it all home?" asks your wife. It is no problem.
The AMI 8 even has room for the Christmas tree. It gets dark. You Drive home. The strong headlights of the AMI 8 light up the street. The windshield wipers keep your view free from snow.
In the AMI 8 you have an excellent view all around. Through the big front and rear windows and six side windows.
Nothing escapes your view.

DER TAG, AN DEM MAN HAUSEINWEIHUNG FEIERT

Der Tag, an dem man zum ersten Mal in seinem neuen Haus wohnt. Der Tag, an dem alle Träume von Komfort und Behaglichkeit wahr werden. Sie haben Freunde eingeladen. Das Feuer knistert im Kamin. Alle sind begeistert und beneiden Sie um Ihr Glück.

Ein AMI 8 - ein Fest.

Sie haben ihn vor dem Haus geparkt, und seine Chromteile blitzen in der Sonne. Für sie ist er auch ein neues Haus.

Die Kinder spielen darin. Und im Grunde sind Sie vielleicht ebenso stolz auf Ihren AMI 8 wie auf Ihr neues Heim.

Citroën hat den Komfort seiner Automobile ständig erhöht. Beim AMI 8 wurde lediglich die Radaufhängung des Vorgängers (AMI 6) übernommen - sie war schon perfekt.

Heizung und Lüftung wurden verbessert.

Die Beinfreiheit vor den Rücksitzen wurde vergrößert.

In den Türfüllungen wurden Ablagen und Armlehnen angebracht. Das ist zeitgemäßer Komfort.

The "big flap" of the Ami 8. For its price, the car offered enormous utility and was considered thrifty and robust. But the great breakthrough was denied it all the same.

THE DAY ON WHICH ONE CELEBRATES HOUSEWARMING.

The day on which one first lives in one's new house. The day on which all one's dreams of comfort and coziness come true. You have invited friends. The fire crackles in the fireplace. Everyone is excited and envies you your happiness.

An AMI 8—a celebration.

You parked it in front of the house, and its chrome parts glisten in the sun.

The children play in it. For them too, it is a new house.

The children are right. And basically, you are just as proud of your AMI 8 as of your new home.

Citroën has constantly increased the comfort of its automobiles. In the AMI 8, only the suspension of its forerunner (the AMI 6) was retained—it was already perfect.

Heating and ventilation were improved.

The legroom in front of the rear seats was increased.

Pockets and armrests were added in the door linings. That is contemporary comfort.

The Little Goddess: Dyane

At first the rumor went around that the Dyane would replace the 2 CV. In fact, the car, introduced in Paris in 1967, did represent a modernized Duck in many ways, but it had only 425 cc and 18.5 HP, and like the Ami 6 or 8, this individual little car was not able to attain the popularity of the original Duck. The 2 CV went on being built, while the Dyane—with a succession of new modifications—lasted until 1982.

A simple brochure page for the new Dyane, of which the text said it had settled between the 2 CV and the Ami 6—the car had "inherited" much from both.

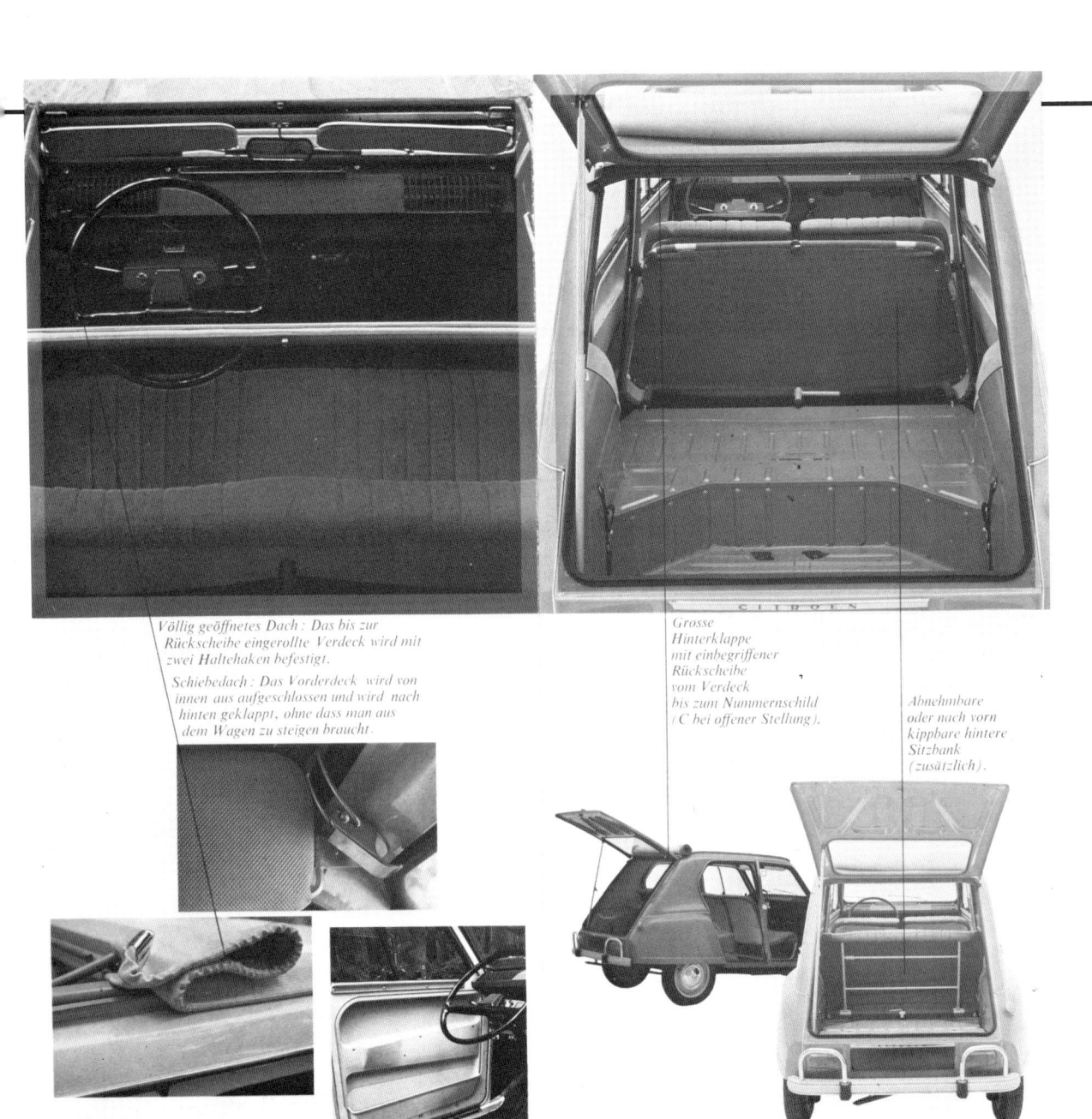

Völlig geöffnetes Dach: Das bis zur Rückscheibe eingerollte Verdeck wird mit zwei Haltehaken befestigt.

Schiebedach: Das Vorderdeck wird von innen aus aufgeschlossen und wird nach hinten geklappt, ohne dass man aus dem Wagen zu steigen braucht.

Grosse Hinterklappe mit einbegriffener Rückscheibe vom Verdeck bis zum Nummernschild (C bei offener Stellung).

Abnehmbare oder nach vorn kippbare hintere Sitzbank (zusätzlich).

Fully opened roof: the top, rolled back to the rear panel, is fastened with two holding hooks.
Sliding roof: The front roof is opened from inside and folded backward, without one's needing to get out of the car.
Large rear hatch with built-in rear window, from the roof to the license plate (C in open position).
Rear seat can be removed or folded forward (optional).

Left: Inner pages of the folding Dyane brochure also shown on page 71.

Right: Naturally one did not have to wait long for a more powerful version of the Dyane. This Dyane 6 brochure dates from the autumn of 1968.

1968

Perfect photography again in
this case. This Dyane catalog is
graphically best-equipped.

For a change, another Citroën advertisement in comic-book style. Some illustrations correspond exactly to those in the 2 CV brochure on page 51.

For those who don't want to open the car's engine hood: Under the hood nothing ever happens. The motor runs smoothly at 7000 rpm.
For those who always thought front drive was better than a rear engine: The Dyane fulfills all your wishes.
For those who want to drive without problems. The four well-balanced gears make driving a pleasure, both in the city and on country roads.
For those who don't always want to be passed: The Dyane cruises at 120 kph.
The Dyane is for those who don't want to have troubles with their car. The Dyane has a simple and long-proven motor of 602 cc. The electric system is extremely simple: failures are no longer possible. The dynamo is replaced by an alternator: no trouble starting. The Dyane doesn't spend any time at the garage.

Für diejenigen, die die Motorhaube des Wagens nicht öffnen wollen : Unter der Motorhaube des Dyane geschieht nie etwas. Der Motor läuft reibungslos mit 7.000 U/Min.

Für diejenigen, die immer dachten, der Vorderradantrieb sei besser als der Heckmotor : der Dyane erfüllt alle ihre Wünsche.

Für diejenigen, die ohne Geschichten fahren wollen : Die vier gut ausgeglichenen Gänge machen das Fahren sowohl in der Stadt wie auf Ueberlandstrassen zum Vergnügen.

Der Dyane ist für diejenigen, die mit ihrem Wagen keine Sorgen haben wollen. Der Dyane hat einen einfachen und seit langem bewährten Motor von 602 cm³. Die elektrische Anlage ist äusserst einfach : Pannen sind nicht mehr möglich. Der Dynamo wird durch einen Alternator ersetzt : keine Sorgen beim Anlassen. Nichts mehr einzustellen. Der Dyane kennt keine Aufenthalte in der Garage.

Für diejenigen, die nicht immer überholt werden wollen : Der Dyane fährt mit 120 km/Std.

Citroën Méhari

A small open all-purpose vehicle on the basis of the 2 CV was equipped with the name of a North African camel: Méhari. Because of its soft plastic body, which was regarded as easily inflammable, this car suffered many limitations from officialdom outside France. The Méhari was totally washable, and when it was dented, the bent spot sprang back into shape...

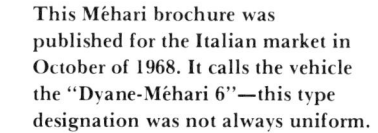

This Méhari brochure was published for the Italian market in October of 1968. It calls the vehicle the "Dyane-Méhari 6"—this type designation was not always uniform.

Inside pages of the brochure shown at left. The roof construction was basically superfluous, because in any case the wind and rain came into the car from all sides in bad weather.

1969

Méhari brochure page in German, from August 1969. Only a few examples—mostly by private means—were imported into Germany and authorized individually.

La Méhari

And then came a somewhat improved and more comfortable version of the Méhari. Among other things, a centrifugal clutch was available—as well as a version without a dashboard.

1972

CARACTÉRISTIQUES
Cylindrée 602 cm3.
Refroidissement à air.
Puissance fiscale 3 CV.
Puissance 33 ch. SAE à 7000 tr/mn.
Pneus 135/380 X.
Coloris : Rouge, Vert, Orange, Ocre.

Il faut se souvenir que la Méhari est une sorte de chameau : elle peut transporter 400 kg et n'a besoin que de très peu d'essence.
Il faut encore se souvenir que la Méhari est une sorte de rhinocéros ; elle ne craint pas les chocs.
Il faut enfin se souvenir que la Méhari est une sorte de voiture.
Mais bien plus amusante.

2 modèles

Version 2 places + 2

Type de base
Pare-brise rabattable en alliage
Chaînes de sécurité. Dais coto
Armature tubulaire avec les 2
milieu recouverts en ABS.
Banquette arrière amovible et

1ère Option
Capotage complet. Bas de p
supérieure en toile et vinyle
latéraux transparents (1100
Options "ENAC" sur Méha
Capote repliable en coton
ou en ABS. Hard-top en AI
Portes avec ou sans glaces.

Autres options
Embrayage centrifuge. Pn

Pas de taxe sur les voitures de

The last word: Méhari
with four-wheel drive,
introduced in May of 1979.

LA MEHARI SERIEUSEMENT

La Méhari est puissante.
Elle a un vaillant moteur de 3 CV qui développe 33 ch. Cela lui confère une puissance importante car elle est légère ; c'est ce qui lui permet de se déplacer n'importe où : sur route, dans un chemin de campagne, aussi bien que dans le désert. Qui peut en faire autant ? Peu !
La Méhari est économique.

Pour les loisirs, son système de climatisation (chauffage-dégivrage) permet de voyager aussi agréablement en été qu'en hiver. Pour le travail, elle est suffisamment robuste pour transporter 400 kg.
Ce qui est beaucoup pour une si gentille voiture. Brave Méhari !

Son moteur est refroidi par air : donc pas de joints, pas de durites ; donc moins de risques d'usure. Il est robuste et d'une conception très simple ; donc moins de pannes ; donc moins de séjours au garage ; donc moins de frais d'entretien ; donc plus d'argent dans votre porte-monnaie ; donc plus de satisfaction.
La Méhari est rationnelle.

81

CITROËN
MEHARI 4×4

ANNÉE MODÈLE 1980

Title page of a July 1979 four-wheel-drive brochure. The rear drive can be switched off; there are disc brakes on all wheels.

Detailed pictures of the Méhari 4x4. Outside of France this vehicle was only seen frequently in North Africa—in Central Europe the four-wheel-drive vehicle is definitely a rarity.

Citroën Méhari Azur

La Citroën Méhari Azur, la voiture "plein air" par excellence, est un véhicule différent des autres. Elle est destinée aux automobilistes pour qui la conduite est un véritable plaisir.
Pratique, fiable et élégante, la Méhari Azur fait preuve d'une extraordinaire polyvalence. D'une quatre places, elle se transforme en deux places avec une très grande capacité de chargement grâce à la banquette arrière escamotable. La capote se démonte facilement pour mieux profiter du soleil. En plus, une grande poche "kangourou" sous le toit abrite les éléments supérieurs de portillons.

Une mécanique à la hauteur

La Méhari Azur est équipée d'un moteur refroidi par air avec carburateur double corps qui développe 29 ch DIN (puissance fiscale 3 CV). La consommation est de 7,5 litres aux 100 km à 90 km/h (vitesse stabilisée) et de 6,8 litres aux 100 km en parcours urbain. La stabilité est assurée grâce à la traction avant et à une suspension à quatre roues indépendantes. Côté sécurité, la Méhari Azur est équipée de freins à disque à l'avant.

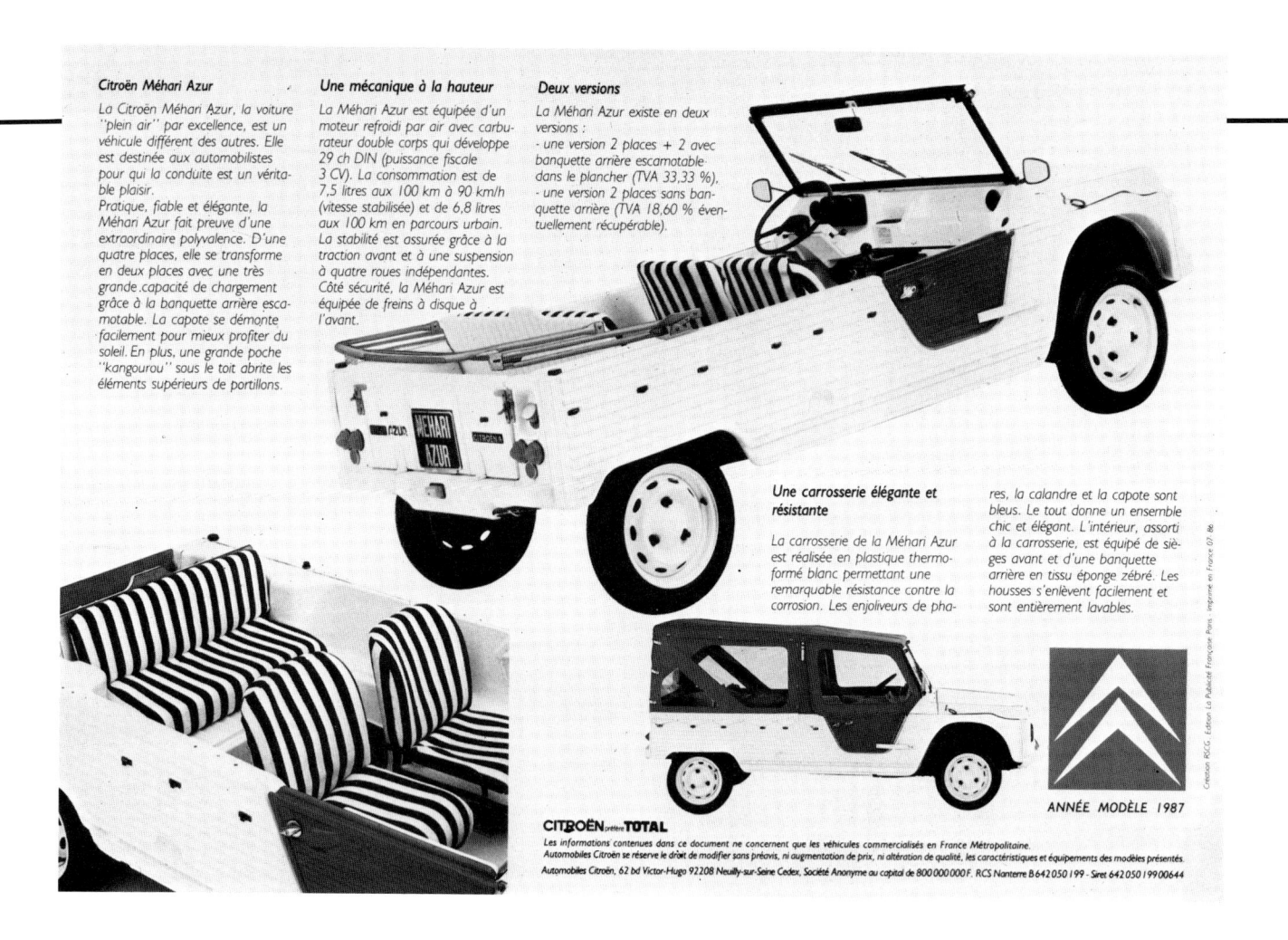

Deux versions

La Méhari Azur existe en deux versions :
- une version 2 places + 2 avec banquette arrière escamotable dans le plancher (TVA 33,33 %),
- une version 2 places sans banquette arrière (TVA 18,60 % éventuellement récupérable).

Une carrosserie élégante et résistante

La carrosserie de la Méhari Azur est réalisée en plastique thermoformé blanc permettant une remarquable résistance contre la corrosion. Les enjoliveurs de phares, la calandre et la capote sont bleus. Le tout donne un ensemble chic et élégant. L'intérieur, assorti à la carrosserie, est équipé de sièges avant et d'une banquette arrière en tissu éponge zébré. Les housses s'enlèvent facilement et sont entièrement lavables.

CITROËN préfère TOTAL

Les informations contenues dans ce document ne concernent que les véhicules commercialisés en France Métropolitaine. Automobiles Citroën se réserve le droit de modifier sans préavis, ni augmentation de prix, ni altération de qualité, les caractéristiques et équipements des modèles présentés. Automobiles Citroën, 62 bd Victor-Hugo 92208 Neuilly-sur-Seine Cedex, Société Anonyme au capital de 800 000 000 F, RCS Nanterre B 642 050 199 - Siret 642 050 199 00644

ANNÉE MODÈLE 1987

A Méhari brochure page from the autumn of 1986. The vehicle became more elegant, and meanwhile also received a somewhat better roof. The 29-HP motor helped this car reach a sustained speed of 100 kph, and whoever ordered it with only two seats saved half the value-added tax in France.

1976

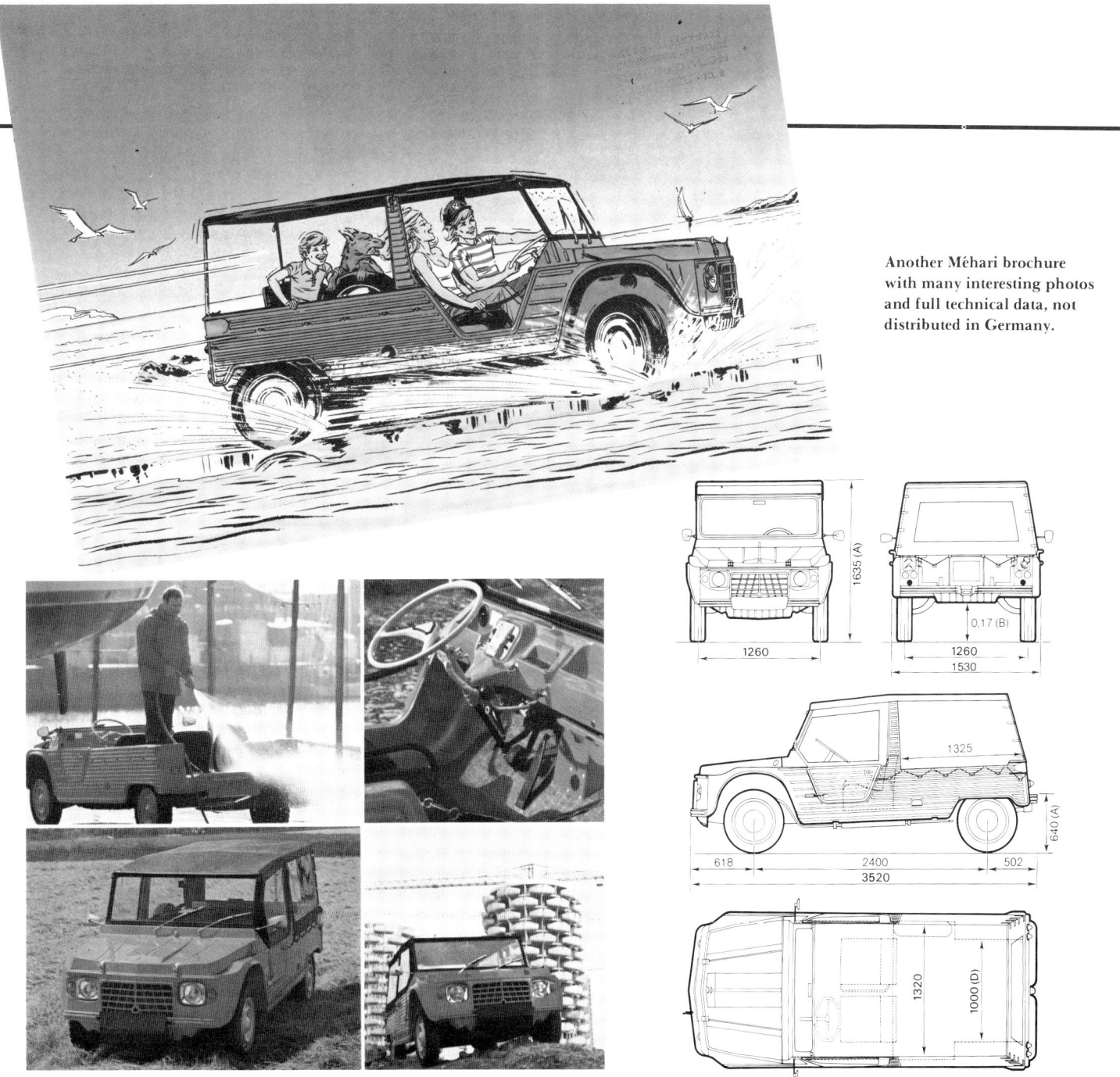

Another Méhari brochure with many interesting photos and full technical data, not distributed in Germany.

The 2 CV in the Press

The "French Lloyd", said the title of a road-test report written by the special reporter of the German magazine *Das Auto*, in which one of the first German-language tests of the Citroën 2 CV appeared at the end of 1950. The Germans were not, though, to enjoy this car until 1958, when exporting began, but this strange car aroused the highest interest everywhere quite early. Full of tension, the tester sat down in the car that had been lent by a French colleague: "I am 1.872 meters tall and weigh a good 90 kilograms, quite a mountain for such a small car. And indeed, the car did go to its knees when I climbed in and let myself down somewhat mistrustfully on the unusual 'hammock seat' behind the wheel. The seats of the 2 CV, front and rear alike, consist of a steel tube frame, to which the seat and back panels of heavy cloth are fastened by rubber strips. But it turned out that one can sit on them very nicely."

In fact, the roominess of the 2 CV, remarkably good for such a small car, amazed the tester, and the primitive but effective and practical details of the furnishings soon made him forget the remarkable appearance. The tester had no illusions about the performance of the 9-HP four-seater:

"As was not to be expected otherwise with a power-to-weight ratio of 50 kg/HP and an engine of only two cylinders, driving the Citroën '2 CV' amounts to shifting, shifting and more shifting. Thanks to the fully synchronized gearbox this is no problem at all for even the most untalented driver. For city streets and normal highways, third gear is enough. At more than 40 kph on the open highway, one shifts into overdrive, which decreases the engine speed in comparison with the speed of the driveshafts by about 30%. The highest speed I reached was 62 kph."

Naturally the suspension, working with longitudinal coil springs and giving the 2 CV the riding comfort of a turnpike cruiser, inspired enthusiasm: "In the neighborhood of Versailles there are a few potholed stretches that demand everything of the suspension. The '2 CV' rolled over them in majestic style all the same, without any hard jolts or the slightest tendency to sway. Even driving over curbstones at 35 to 40 kph did not for a moment disturb its republican-French equilibrium."

After the end of the test drives, the skeptical tester had a lot of respect for this remarkable French creation, even if he still could not come to terms with the form it took:

"When I returned the car in the evening, I had gained a real respect for the 'war horse' and the constructive achievement embodied in it. But the ugly exterior remains. Would it really have cost the manufacturer so much more to have given it a somewhat more appetizing form?—Of course it is probably true that the '2 CV' was designed less for city dwellers than for country folk: Among farmers, vintners, peddlers, small business people etc. the elegance of the outward appearance plays only a very subordinate role."

Left: A 1982 2 CV 6 in "Club" form, a comfortable car that also sold very well in Germany. Right: A Super-Duck from a series of individual cars, turned into a 3-axle vehicle and used for advertising purposes by the makers of Gauloise cigarettes.

The Swiss began to import the smallest Citroën as early as 1952, and so there appeared in the well-known Swiss magazine *Automobil Revue* in the summer of 1953 a detailed test report in the form of a long-distance trial. It began with a compliment: "The result of our long-distance trial with the Citroën 2 CV turned out very favorably for the car. Despite the low engine power and the simple furnishings, it proved to be a solid, pleasant, very versatile and economical car that could please us more and more in the course of the trial. The judgment that the 2 CV is only suitable for around-town and short-haul driving is one that we must definitely oppose."

During the 6000 test kilometers driven on Swiss roads, mountain passes were not avoided, and the little two-cylinder engines's stability and elasticity was surprising: "Mountain and pass roads always require first and second gears, and thus a considerable speed reduction. First gear, with four people on board, is sufficient for grades up to about 20%. Driving up steeper grades, such as occur very rarely on major roads but more often on smaller second and third-class roads in the foothills of the Alps, is not possible with a fully loaded car. Our big pass highways, on the other hand, offer no difficulties. Thanks to the good synchronizing of the gears, any loss of time in shifting can be avoided. One can also drive for some time on grades in the lower gears at full throttle without damaging the engine."

The Swiss were also very enthusiastic about the revolutionary suspension of the 2 CV: "The roadholding is so excellent that one never has the feeling of coming even close to the edge of safety. On sharp curves, surprisingly, one leaves many another car behind. But when one observes the 2 CV from outside during fast cornering, the strong tilting of the body looks downright threatening. Meanwhile the passengers notice nothing of it, and the driver feels a particular security in a curve. That is especially true of taking curves while giving some gas."

The interior furnishings were found to be very simple but purposeful and quite comfortable: "The access to all four seats is very good. One does not climb down into the car, as is customary today, but just sits down on a chair. The height of the doors allows one to get in with one's hat on one's head."

Typ	2 CV A	2 CV AV	2 CV AZ/AZLP	2 CV AZV	2 CV 4X4 Sahara
Baujahr	1948 – 1954	1951 – 1954	1954 – 1959	1954 – 1959	1958 – 1959
Bohrung x Hub mm	62 x 62	62 x 62	66 x 62	66 x 62	66 x 62
Hubraum cm^3	375	375	425	425	425
Leistung PS bei U/min.	9 bei 3500	9 bei 3500	12 bei 3500	12 bei 3500	2 x 12 bei 3500
max. Drehmoment mkg bei U/min	2 bei 2000	2 bei 2000	2,2 bei 2000	2,2 bei 2000	2 x 2,4 bei 2500
Verdichtung	6,2 : 1	6,2 : 1	6,2 : 1	6,2 : 1	7 : 1
Vergaser	Fallstrom SOLEX 22 Z ACI	Fallstrom SOLEX 22 Z ACI	Fallstrom SOLEX 26 BCI	Fallstrom SOLEX 26 BCI	SOLEX 26 CBIN
Batterie	6 Volt/50 Ah	6 Volt/50 Ah	6 Volt/50 Ah	6 Volt/50 Ah	6 Volt/60 Ah
Radstand mm	2370	2370	2370	2370	2405
Spur v./h. mm	1260	1260	1260	1260	1260
Länge x Breite x Höhe mm	3780 x 1480 x 1600	3600 x 1500 x 1700	3780 x 1480 x 1600	3600 x 1500 x 1700	3780 x 1460 x 1540
Leergewicht kg	495	515	495	515	735
Zul. Gesamtgewicht kg	800	835	800	835	1040
Höchstgeschwindigkeit km/h	65	60	70	65	100 (mit beiden Motoren)
Verbrauch Liter/100 km	4,5	5	5	5,5	6 – 12 (mit 1 oder 2 Motoren)

The potential for being loaded with a good deal of luggage also surprised the testers; the only thing they missed was an interior light, for at night one cannot read the speedometer. In the end, the little Citroën was described as follows: "The Citroën 2 CV was not meant for the long-distance driver or the snob; it is rather the best realization to date of a vehicle with optimal performance and minimal operating costs. The manufacturer has been generous in just one area: namely in the richness of original and practical ideas that the 2 CV incorporates. It can fulfill its task in its present form for years to come."

In a 1954 test by the English magazine *Light Car*, praise is given first of all to the excellent access to all the components under the engine hood; then the driver takes his seat:

"The interior space of the 2 CV is surprising. The first impression that one gets when one has sat down behind the stable two-spoke steering wheel is that the springs have sagged a lot; then one notices how much room is available, in front and in back. Third, the seats prove to be very particularly comfortable."

The engine, though not exactly strong as a bear, pleased the testers, as is did the easy-to-shift gearbox: "The engine is not exactly quiet, to be sure, but the ear soon gets used to its healthy sound, and one senses, almost unconsciously, the right moment to shift gears, The car is built so that one almost always drives it on full throttle, for on upgrades the car loses its verve immediately. Quick downshifting is then the most important thing."

In August of 1958 the magazine *Der Kleinwagen* published its experiences with the 2 CV, now producing 12.5 HP. But the power increase was not enough to suit the tester: "One can be driven to despair when one chugs up medium-sized mountains

Typ	2 CV AZ/AZLP	2 CV AZU/AZLP	2 CV 4x4 Sahara	2 CV AZV	2 CV AZ; AZA; AZAM
Baujahr	1959 – 1960	1959 – 1962/63	1959 – 1965	1962 – 1963	1963 – 1969
Bohrung x Hub mm	66 x 62	66 x 62	66 x 62	66 x 62	66 x 62
Hubraum cm^3	425	425	425	425	425
Leistung PS bei U/min.	12,5 bei 4200	12,5 (13,5) bei 4200	2 x 12,5 bei 4200	13,5 bei 4000	16,5 bei 4200
max. Drehmoment mkg bei U/min	2,4 bei 2500	2,4 bei 2500	2 x 2,4 bei 2500	2,7 bei 2500	2,75 bei 2500
Verdichtung	7 : 1	7 : 1	7 : 1	7 : 1	7 : 1
Vergaser	SOLEX 26 BCI	SOLEX 26 BCI	SOLEX 26 BCI	SOLEX 26 CBI oder IBC	SOLEX 28 CBI oder IBC
Batterie	6 Volt/50 Ah	6 Volt/50 Ah	6 Volt/60 Ah	6 Volt/60 Ah	6 Volt/60 Ah
Radstand mm	2370	2370	2405	2370	2370
Spur v./h. mm	1260	1260	1260	1260	1260
Länge x Breite x Höhe mm	3780 x 1480 x 1600	3600 x 1500 x 1700	3780 x 1460 x 1540	3600 x 1500 x 1700	3780 x 1480 x 1600
Leergewicht kg	495	515 (495)	735	515	495
Zul. Gesamtgewicht kg	830	835 (830)	1040	835	830
Höchstgeschwindigkeit km/h	70	65 (85)	100 (2 Motoren)	65	95
Verbrauch Liter/100 km	5	5,5	6 – 12	6	6

with this four-wheeled Ju 52 and easily passes the greater percentage of the other vehicles on the road. Third gear is often no longer up to the task, and in second one has to more or less overrev the engine to be able to keep rolling. Here the 12.5 HP are used up, leaving us lacking that which was lost in deliberate detuning to attain robustness and economy. After the other excellent characteristics, one simply expects more; whether one is allowed to expect more is another matter!" The test car was equipped with the centrifugal clutch, which simplified 2 CV maintenance even more:

"The high point of the 2 CV is the dry clutch with centrifugal regulation, in which no torque is transmitted under 1000 rpm. Thus it is possible to stop in 4th, 3rd, 2nd or 1st gear without declutching and—what is really sensational: the car can be put back into motion (in any gear!!) without using the clutch. Naturally starting in 3rd or 4th gear is not recommended. All gears are synchronized and really soft as butter to shift. Only when shifting from 2nd to 1st gear does one need to double-clutch."

One of the most fascinating 2 CV types, the twin-engined 4x4 "Sahara", was introduced to the press in 1959 at Mer de sable, a proving ground for military vehicles not far from Paris, and the tester from *Motor Rundschau* had a chance to try out the all-wheel Duck:

"This vehicle is intended for the Sahara, for example, and has already gained a nickname: the mechanical donkey! When driving down the same slopes that one had just climbed, one does not have the unpleasant sensation of falling into an abyss, as was the case with previously known vehicles—built with bone-hard springs for military purposes. This is because the passengers are not exposed to hard

Typ	2 CV AK	2 CV AZU	2 CV 4x4 Sahara	2 CV AZAM	2 CV AZV	2 CV 4 (Special)
Baujahr	1963 – 1968	1963 – 1967	1965 – 1967	1966	1967 – 1969	1970 – 1978
Bohrung x Hub mm	74 x 70	66 x 62	66 x 62	74 x 70	66 x 62	68,5 x 59
Hubraum cm^3	597	425	425	597	425	435
Leistung PS bei U/min.	21 bei 4500	16,5 bei 4200	2 x 16,5 bei 4200	21 bei 4500	18 bei 5450	24 bei 6750
max. Drehmoment mkg bei U/min	3,75 bei 3000	2,75 bei 2500	2 x 2,75 bei 2500	3,75 bei 3000	3 bei 3500	2,9 bei 4000
Verdichtung	7,25 : 1	7 : 1	7 : 1	7,25 : 1	7,25 : 1	85 : 1
Vergaser	SOLEX 30 PBI	ZENITH 28 IN oder SOLEX 26 IBC	SOLEX 26 CBI oder 28 IBC	SOLEX 30 PBI	SOLEX 32 PICS	SOLEX 32 PCIS 4
Batterie	6 Volt/60 Ah	6 Volt/60 Ah	6 Volt/60 Ah	12 Volt/30 Ah	12 Volt/30 Ah	12 Volt/25 Ah
Radstand mm	2370	2370	2405	2370	2370	2370
Spur v./h. mm	1260	1260	1260	1260	1260	1260
Länge x Breite x Höhe mm	3600 x 1500 x 1700	3600 x 1500 x 1700	3780 x 1460 x 1540	3780 x 1480 x 1600	3600 x 1500 x 1700	3780 x 1480 x 1600
Leergewicht kg	605	515	735	495	515	560
Zul. Gesamtgewicht kg	1030	835	1040	830	835	895
Höchstgeschwindigkeit km/h	98	95	115	100	98	102
Verbrauch Liter/100 km	8	6	6,5 – 12,5	6	6	5,4

jolts and the changes of speed in various directions are somewhat subdued."

In 1963—the already venerable 2 CV had meanwhile gotten a new injection of power and now attained a proud 16 HP—the magazine *Mot* had the chance to test the newest "Luxe" model, which offered such accessories as automatic interior lighting, two sun visors, thickly upholstered seats and a lot of chrome, doing honor to the "luxury" designation for a 2 CV. But in spite of its noticeable improvements, the tester had various reasons for not advising anyone to buy such a car:

"On upgrades it loses speed quickly, it backs up traffic behind it, and that can easily make the driver nervous. He has to deal with problems, has little reserve power for passing, and it gets dangerous then, for he laboriously fights his way forward in the passing lane once he pulls out without power at low speed. Thus one must unfortunately come to the conclusion that for present conditions in Germany the Ami 6 is what the 2 CV cannot be, to say nothing of the (Renault) R 4. It is also true that for German conditions the 2 CV may be extraordinarily thrifty (we drove over 250 km at a bit over 65 kph and consumed only 5.0 liters; as a yearly average, more than 6.5 liters simply does not occur, even under unfavorable conditions), but the so beautifully simple body and chassis spare parts are not as cheap as for the 2 CV at home, and the repair shops sometimes treat it with contempt."

But even at this time there were already numerous fans of this vehicle that was so different from other

Typ	2 CV 6	2 CV AKS 400	2 CV 6	2 CV 6 (Special); Club; Charleston
Baujahr	1970–1975	1970–1975	1975–1978	1978–
Bohrung x Hub mm	74 x 70	74 x 70	74 x 70	74 x 70
Hubraum cm³	602	602	602	602
Leistung PS bei U/min.	28,5 bei 5750	21 bei 4500	26 bei 5500	29 bei 5750
max. Drehmoment mkg bei U/min	4 bei 3500	3,75 bei 3000	4 bei 3500	4 bei 3500
Verdichtung	8,5 : 1	7,25 : 1	8,5 : 1	8,5 : 1
Vergaser	SOLEX 34 PCIS 4	SOLEX 30 PBI	SOLEX 34 PICS 6	SOLEX 26/35
Batterie	12 Volt/25 Ah	12 Volt/25 Ah	12 Volt/25 Ah	12 Volt/25 Ah
Radstand mm	2370	2370	2370	2370
Spur v./h. mm	1260	1260	1260	1260
Länge x Breite x Höhe mm	3780 x 1480 x 1600	3805 x 1500 x 1840	3780 x 1480 x 1600	3780 x 1480 x 1600
Leergewicht kg	560	640	560	560
Zul. Gesamtgewicht kg	895	1115	895	895
Höchstgeschwindigkeit km/h	110	85	108	110
Verbrauch Liter/100 km	6,5	7,5	6,1	6,1

cars, and they could rejoice at its higher performance:

"Technically the most cheering thing about the new model is that the engine obviously provides more acceleration and a somewhat higher top speed; see the figures and acceleration curve in the technical data. Despite the increased performance, the engine is exactly as healthy as before, and the fuel consumption is somewhat higher only under extreme use. The gear ratios were reduced a bit, to provide more speed in comparison to the engine speed—thus one must shift somewhat more than before, especially in a heavily loaded car."

Meanwhile the Citroën "Ami 6", a sort of noble 2 CV with a very eccentric body, came on the market here. *Mot* published a test report the next year. Though the car looked remarkable at first sight, a closer observation revealed many well-planned details: "Original, somewhat extravagant, but absolutely elegant styling of the individual parts (sheet metal parts, headlights) as of the whole, along with the greatest refinement of the furnishings: roundings and profilings serve to stiffen the thin sheet metal, resulting in a light body. Window frames are simply bent profile material, the grille is a simple screen, the most extreme simplicity, even in the bumpers—but still with over-riders and rubber pads. The wide edge of the roof holds the upper body together solidly, for the roof is made of plastic."

The interior decor also pleased the tester: "The plastic roof is somewhat transparent, the sides with well-applied imitation leather coverings, the very smooth dashboard with a bit of gold on the knobs, sheet metal with iron-oxide paint, some imitation leather on the lower rim, projecting instrument carriers, free-standing steering wheel on the bent column—everything is smart and easy and practical."

Typ	ACADIANE	AMI 6	AMI 6	AMI 6	AMI 8
Baujahr	1978 –	1961 – 1963	1963 – 1967	1967 – 1969	1969 – 1967
Bohrung x Hub mm	74 x 70	74 x 70	74 x 70	74 x 70	74 x 70
Hubraum cm³	602	602	602	602	602
Leistung PS bei U/min.	31 bei 5750	21 bei 4500	24,5 bei 4750	28 bei 5750	32 bei 5750
max. Drehmoment mkg bei U/min	4,2 bei 3500	4,1 bei 2800	4,1 bei 3000	4,1 bei 3000	4,2 bei 4000
Verdichtung	8,5 : 1	7,25 : 1	7,75 : 1	8,5 : 1	9 : 1
Vergaser	SOLEX 26 x 35 CSIC	SOLEX 30 PBI	SOLEX 30 PBI	SOLEX 34 PCIS 4	SOLEX 36 x 35 CSIC
Batterie	12 Volt/25 Ah	12 Volt/25 Ah	12 Volt/25 Ah	12 Volt/25 Ah	12 Volt/30 Ah
Radstand mm	2535	2400	2400	2400	2400
Spur v./h. mm	1260	1260/1220	1260/1220	1260/1220	1260/1220
Länge x Breite x Höhe mm	4030 x 1500 x 1825	3960 x 1520 x 1490	3960 x 1520 x 1490	3960 x 1520 x 1490	3990 x 1520 x 1490
Leergewicht kg	680	640	640	640	725
Zul. Gesamtgewicht kg	1155	980	980	980	1050
Höchstgeschwindigkeit km/h	100	105	112	115	120
Verbrauch Liter/100 km	7,5	6	6,3	6,5	6,5

The controls stood out by their sensible location and ease of use, and the suspension spoiled the passengers even more than that of the 2 CV, since hydraulic shock absorbers prevented this model from swaying all too easily. The 2 CV philosophy prevailed in the quality of workmanship:

"The Ami 6 is built with uttermost simplicity. Simple parts are simply assembled. What is important (powerplant and chassis) is good and very accurate; everything else is regarded as not so important. But one should not let oneself be irritated by details that may at first seem crude and primitive: here the ideal of the simplest automobile is realized, and one sees again and again that the important things are really good."

So in the end the total judgment was naturally good, but in the meantime there arose several competitors, and buying an Ami in Germany turned out to be the exception:

"The Citroën Ami 6 always impresses us in its way when we have contact with it. Its absolute driving safety, the high degree of comfort and the functional elegance of its furnishings add up to a lot. Yet making a decision to buy it is difficult. Above all, because of the Renault R 4, which is built more as a utilitarian car inside and out, but is stronger, quieter, practical in many ways and above all, a lot less expensive."

In 1971 there was at last a choice between the 2 CV 4 and 2 CV 6 models. The magazine *Auto, Motor und Sport* tested the more powerful model thoroughly. This Duck, with its 28 HP, was a real rocket compared to earlier examples of the type, and with its top speed of 111 kph, it even allowed the testers to measure its acceleration from 0 to 100 kph, the time of 31.6 seconds being even better than that of the contemporary Austin Mini 850—who would ever have expected that from a 2 CV?

"Too much applause would have been superfluous, though, for even 28 horsepower are not very much, in absolute terms, for a car weighing 600 kilograms. Yet one must say that the earlier days of driving a 2 CV in a constant state of modesty are definitely at an end. The clattering two-cylinder engine, loud as a sport airplane at high engine speeds, accelerated the thin-walled car to 80 kph in 16.1 seconds and to 100 kph in 31.6 seconds, with which one cannot play a dominant role but can get along well in traffic flow. In most cases one is even faster than the average overland traffic when one fully utilizes the engines's power up to over 7000 rpm, and can scarcely avoid passing."

Otherwise nothing important had changed about the Duck over the course of time. One simply had to have the right attitude to be happy with this car: "Exposed door hinges cause as little disturbance in the French cheap-car class as primitive interior decor or luggage space lined in bare metal. And whoever is horrified at watching the door lock do its job is obviously just a bit too aesthetic."

This time the outstanding winter handling characteristics were especially praised: "The Citroën, with Michelin X tires of 125-15 size as standard equipment, proves to be a real master of snowy roads and climbs steep slopes with these tires, where conventionally built cars have trouble even with spiked tires. Driving over any ridges of snow that remain in the middle of the road before the final thaw is also problem-free; unimpressed by suddenly arising hindrances, the 2 CV can be held cleanly on the track and steered with the necessary precision." And: "After one has forced oneself through the narrow door and sat down on the very sympathetic seats, one feels little desire to get out soon. And comfort is provided in other ways too: Air can be let into the interior of the car in all imaginable places, by the roll-up roof that can be fastened in two positions, by a wide inlet at dashboard level, and finally by those typical hinged windows that are as characteristic of this car as the shape of its fenders."

These judgments have basically not lost their validity to this day, for this unusual car still finds friends all over the world.

Typ	DYANE	DYANE 4	DYANE 6	DYANE 6	MÉHARI/MÉHARI 4X4
Baujahr	1967 – 1968	1968 – 1974	1968 – 1970	1970 – 1983	1968 –
Bohrung x Hub mm	66 x 62	68,5 x 59	74 x 70	74 x 70	
Hubraum cm³	425	435	602	602	
Leistung PS bei U/min.	18,5 bei 4750	24 bei 7000	28 bei 5750	32 bei 5750	
max. Drehmoment mkg bei U/min	3 bei 3500	3 bei 4000	4 bei 3500	4,2 bei 4000	Entwicklung wie bei DYANE/2 CV
Verdichtung	7,25 : 1	8,5 : 1	8,5 : 1	8,5 : 1	
Vergaser	SOLEX 32 PICS	SOLEX 32 PCIS 4	SOLEX 34 PCIS 4	SOLEX 36 x 35 CSIC	
Batterie	12 Volt/30 Ah	12 Volt/30 Ah	12 Volt/30 Ah	12 Volt/30 Ah	
Radstand mm	2370	2370	2370	2370	2370/2570
Spur v./h. mm	1260	1260	1260	1260	1260
Länge x Breite x Höhe mm	3900 x 1500 x 1540	3900 x 1500 x 1540	3900 x 1500 x 1540	3900 x 1500 x 1540	3520 x 1530 x 1635 / 3720 x 1530 x 1635
Leergewicht kg	605	610	610	625	570/735
Zul. Gesamtgewicht kg	925	925	930	930	955/1145
Höchstgeschwindigkeit km/h	95	102	116	118	90 – 100
Verbrauch Liter/100 km	6	6	6,2	6,4	6,8 – 9

Text continued from page 11.

platform chassis, suspension, steering and engine as the 2 CV, though the engine had been enlarged to 602 cc, for this heavy car and at first produced 22 HP (24.5 as of 1963). Typical of Citroën in the Ami was the unusual body, rejected by many as too extravagant, with its wide roof tilting backward, not to mention its front hood. The body had a very "tinny" appearance but offered a lot of space and comfort inside.

Ami-6 production ended in 1969 with the introduction of the Ami 8 with its cutoff tail and clearly improved interior, a car that stayed in production as a sedan and wagon until 1978, the line being expanded in 1973 by the Ami Super, with the 1015-cc engine of the Citroën GS, which was built for only two years.

The "Dyane" type that debuted in Paris in 1967 was originally supposed to replace the Duck, but this 2 CV in modernized attire scarcely provided competition for the old model; it offered the Duck's advantages in a purely technical sense and in terms of utility, but whereas the Duck was ugly but highly original, one could unfortunately not say the same of the Dyane. In spite of that, the Dyane, with the old 425-cc engine at first upgraded to 18.5 HP, sold very well, especially after the new 435or 602-cc engines were available for the Dyane 4 and Dyane 6 models. In 1970, both gained a third side window and, along with small improvements and optical retouchings, acquired front disc brakes as of 1977. In 1982 production ended in France; there was also a box van version of this model, as well as a few special versions, such as the dark blue "Caban", the yellow and black "Capra" from Spain and the white "Côite d'Azur" model with blue stripes.

Literature for the 2 CV

Das grosse Entenbuch—Der 2 CV by Jürgen Lewandowski and Nikolaus Reichert. Everything about the legendary Duck, its history and its mutations, the most exciting races and trips, the home-built types and all technical changes since production began. 120 b/w photos, 80 color photos on 32 color pages. German text.

Citroën 2 CV—The Ugly Duckling? by Ernst von Altena. A loving observation of the versatile service of this original type of car as ship of the desert, mountain climber, arctic explorer etc. 112 pages, 150 illustrations in color and b/w, English text.

Alles über den Citroën 2 CV by M. Breuninger and E. U. Orlopp. Models from 1948 to 1984, development, data and statistics, accessories, campers and much more. 296 pages, 104 illustrations, German text.

Rund um die Welt im 2 CV by Baudot and Séguéla. Real-life motoring adventure from the Fifties, reprint of an out-of-print book. 210 pages, 30 illustrations, German text.

The Citroën 2 CV and Derivates: A Collector Guide by J. Taylor. A detailed book, covering every model variation thoroughly, with competition results, information for restoration and repair. 128 pages, 127 illustrations, English text.

The Life and Times of the Citroën 2 CV by Bob MacQueen and Julian McNamara. Not so much a complete history of the type as a song of praise to the beloved Duck. 159 pages, 202 illustrations, 12 in color, English text.

Deux Chevaux. A picture book in color, showing lovingly painted Ducks. 84 pages, 62 color photos.

Collection Auto-Archives: In this series several volumes on the Citroën firm have appeared. Every A4 format volume approximately 100 pages, many illustrations, French text. Series includes **Citroën 2 CV 1948-2000?**

Citroën 2 CV 1948-82. A Brooklands Publication with reprints of contemporary road tests and reports. A4 format, 100 pages, very many illustrations, English text.

Ich baue mir eine Reiseente by G. Schmidt. In the Do-it-yourself series is this rebuilding guide for the Duck caravan. A4 format, 58 pages, many b/w illustrations.

Citroën 2 CV 4/2 CV 6. AK 250, AK 400 (to autumn 1975). Bucheli Repair Manual No. 260.

Citroën 2 CV, Ami & Dyane 2-Cyl. 1967-1986. Haynes Repair Manual No. 340.

Citroën 2 CV/Dyane (2 CV 6, Dyane 6)/Me/hari 10/75-7/79. Bucheli Repair Manual No. 340.

Citroën 2 CV Dyane alle Modelle. Now I help myself. Korp Volume 12, German text.

Citroën Ami 6. Bucheli Repair Manual No. 78.

Citroën Ami 8. Bucheli Repair Manual No. 192.